D1405995

PRESUMED
GUILTY

What the Jury Never Knew

About Laci Peterson's Murder

and Why Scott Peterson

Should Not Be on Death Row

ATRIA BOOKS

New York   London   Toronto   Sydney

PRESUMED GUILTY

Matt Dalton

with Bonnie Hearn Hill

ATRIA BOOKS
1230 Avenue of the Americas
New York, NY 10020

ISBN-13: 978-0-7432-8695-4
ISBN-10:   0-7432-8695-2

First Atria Books hardcover edition December 2005

10 9 8 7 6 5 4 3 2 1

ATRIA BOOKS is a trademark of Simon & Schuster, Inc.

Manufactured in the United States of America

For information about special discounts for bulk purchases,
please contact Simon & Schuster Special Sales at
1-800-456-6798 or business@simonandschuster.com.

To my father, my teacher, criminal defense lawyer Doug Dalton

CONTENTS

Introduction: The Book That Had to Be Written—Now   1

1 The Case Against Scott Peterson   9

2 Attorney for the Accused   25

3 Crimes in the Neighborhood   53

4 Credible Witnesses   71

5 The Autopsy Report   81

6 Cults and Coincidences   95

7 Satanic Art, Satanic Killings   113

8 Amber Frey: A Motive for Murder?   121

9 The Victims   131

10 A New Defense Team?   139

11 The Trial   147

12 Beyond the Verdict   171

Appendix: Timeline   187

Acknowledgments   193

PRESUMED GUILTY

THE BOOK THAT HAD TO BE WRITTEN—NOW

NOVEMBER 12, 2004, 1:10 P.M.
REDWOOD CITY, CALIFORNIA

The jury moved into the jury box. The packed courtroom waited.

Accused murderer Scott Peterson sat expressionless and still as the court clerk began to read the verdict form.

After 184 witnesses testifying over twenty-three weeks, the closing arguments had been made. Defense attorney Mark Geragos said in his closing arguments that prosecutors had not proven their case.

"But if you hate him, then maybe what they're asking you to

do is just convict him. Don't bother with the five months of evidence," Geragos said. "Don't bother with the fact that the evidence shows clearly that he didn't do this and had absolutely no motive to do this. . . . You're not supposed to just decide this case on whether or not you like Scott Peterson."

Prosecutor Rick Distaso insisted that Peterson was the only one who could have killed his wife. "The best way to look at [the evidence] is like a jigsaw puzzle," he said. "Each piece that I've talked to you about today fits only in one direction, and that is that this man is guilty of murder."

Finally, the court clerk's voice rang out. "We the jury in the above-entitled cause, find the defendant, Scott Lee Peterson, guilty of the crime of the murder of Laci Denise Peterson."

Sharon Rocha, Laci Peterson's mother, sobbed and fell forward in her seat into the arms of her son, Brent. Gasps came from Laci's friends, who'd hurried to Redwood City in time to hear the verdict.

The trial that had begun June 1, 2004, amid promises of witnesses and evidence that never materialized, was over. Scott Peterson had been found guilty. The verdict was first degree for Laci, second degree for her unborn son, Conner.

This was more than another true-crime drama to me. It represented six months of my life, countless hours of investigation, and a sick sense of dread that justice would not prevail because the jury did not have the same information I did.

I never planned to write a book about the Scott Peterson murder trial. Although I left the defense before the case went to trial, I couldn't forget it. After the frustration and disappointment I encountered while working on Peterson's defense team, I wanted to put the entire nightmare behind me. But I couldn't.

The questions would come when I least expected them—sometimes driving down the freeway, sometimes moments before sleep, and always when I picked up a newspaper or watched one of the ubiquitous news broadcasts dissecting the case.

What had happened to the information I'd uncovered about the van that was sitting across from Laci's house the morning of the twenty-fourth and was later seen speeding away from the area where she was last seen walking? The pregnant woman who was being terrorized in the neighborhood? The numerous other pregnant women who'd disappeared in the area? The crime spree in Laci's neighborhood that started hours before she disappeared? The screaming coming from that park bathroom where Laci was seen walking the morning of December 24, 2002? Why was there no testimony from the witnesses I'd interviewed who'd seen Laci with her dog that day? What about the felons who were breaking into the house across the street the morning of December 24?

Why was Scott Peterson on death row?

Those questions continue to haunt me; they are the basis of this book.

JOINING GERAGOS

Over the years that Mark Geragos and I had known each other, we'd talked about working together. I met Mark when I was in college. We were both working for our fathers, well-known criminal defense lawyers who had offices together in the early 1980s. Mark was in law school clerking at the firm. I was an undergraduate student at the University of California, Los Angeles majoring in economics. I worked at the firm part-time doing the payroll and bookkeeping. My father enjoyed great success and managed to retire early from practicing law. Mark later passed the bar, and he and his father began practicing together. After graduating from college, I went to law school and then became a prosecutor.

While working as a Los Angeles County deputy district attorney in February 2001, I began a lengthy, complex investigation into public corruption within the City of Los Angeles. I spent two years on this investigation, using surreptitious electronic devices, interviewing witnesses, and reading through more than one million different documents. I examined every small detail, looking for "the smoking gun," that small piece of information that would prove a crime was being committed. I learned from this experience that a good investigator lives and breathes the facts of his case. That is what I did. Although I didn't know it at the time, it was the perfect preparation for the work I would have to do in the Peterson case.

Very soon after starting this public corruption investigation,

I became focused on one particular area of possible corruption in the City of Los Angeles that I believed should be vigorously pursued. Relationships existed between city officials and contributors in the form of campaign donations in a "pay to play" environment I felt should not be tolerated.

I believed we were closing in on a prosecutable case. However, it was just at this point that Steve Cooley, the Los Angeles district attorney, and a career bureaucrat, decided to end the investigation. I had no idea why.

The *Los Angeles Times* ran a feature article regarding the investigation's termination in which one of its columnists described the situation as "like a chapter from *L.A. Confidential*— a deepening web of political intrigue complete with bribery allegations, bugging devices, a bag man, and a dogged prosecutor turned away by his bosses."

In January 2003, after thirteen years as a career prosecutor involved in all aspects of criminal litigation with the Long Beach City Prosecutor's Office and the Los Angeles County District Attorney's Office, I'd finally had enough.

As I was coming back from hearing Steve Cooley's decision to call off the investigation, I saw Mark Geragos in the hallway at the Criminal Courts Building in downtown Los Angeles. He again asked me when I was going to come work with him and his father.

I was fed up with what I perceived as politics and civil service inertia in the district attorney's office. The offer to go work with the Geragos firm seemed like the perfect solution. It was a possibility that I'd considered for a long time, and now I took him up on it. I had no idea what awaited me as a defense attorney.

Two months after leaving the district attorney's office, I was working full time in Modesto, California, investigating the murder of Laci Peterson. For approximately six months, I worked exclusively on the Peterson case, interviewed scores of witnesses, reviewed the physical facts, and visited the relevant scenes. I thoroughly examined more than thirty thousand pages of police investigation, much of which was unlike any investigative reports I had seen as a Los Angeles prosecutor.

After the guilty verdict in the Peterson case, I was contacted by a member of the press. This person asked me how I felt about the jury's decision and said, "Let me interview you." I was tempted to accept. Although it would have been cathartic just to talk the story out of my system, I knew that it would ultimately do little good.

I didn't want to go on television and argue with lawyers less knowledgeable than I on the facts of the case. In the months I worked on the Peterson murder, I saw many legal commentators relying on erroneous information in stating their opinions on Scott Peterson's guilt. The home audience did not know many of the opinions they were hearing were based on false premises and guesswork.

Conclusions were drawn based on evidence that did not exist. Too much crucial information that did exist was never presented during the trial. I needed to somehow get this message out to an educated audience who might, after learning all the facts, agree there is too much doubt in this case. A television interview is easy to refute; a book, less so.

So here it is, what really happened in the Peterson case: the investigation, the interviews, and the facts that never made it to the courtroom. Regardless of whether or not you agree with the verdict, by the time you finish this book, I think you'll agree that this information might have created a reasonable doubt in the minds of the jurors and may have kept Scott Peterson off death row.

1

THE CASE AGAINST
SCOTT PETERSON

On April 18, 2003, Scott Peterson, a thirty-year-old fertilizer salesman from Modesto, California, was arrested for the murder of his wife, Laci, and their unborn child, whose bodies were identified the same day. Peterson was charged with two counts of murder.

Law enforcement believed that he killed Laci just before Christmas 2002 and dumped her body in San Francisco Bay, three miles from where he said he had been fishing the day she disappeared.

Scott's parents contacted Mark Geragos shortly after their son's arrest, because, his mother explained later to Mark, she had liked him when she watched him on *Larry King Live.*

On Saturday, April 26, 2003, Mark Geragos, investigator Bill Pavelic, and I met with Jackie and Lee Peterson in the downtown Los Angeles offices of Geragos & Geragos. Our meeting took place in the conference room on the thirty-ninth floor of the building. My first impression of the Petersons was that they were articulate, educated, and absolutely sincere in their belief in their son's innocence.

Mark took control of the interview, trying to put the parents of our potential client at ease. "Isn't this a beautiful view?" he began, gesturing toward the windows in the elegant office. He gave some background about the firm, explaining that Geragos & Geragos was made up of several family members and handled civil as well as criminal cases. Finally, he got to the matter at hand and said, "Tell us about this."

That Saturday after their son's arrest, Jackie and Lee Peterson were still in something like a state of shock, yet certain that he would soon be free and that part of the nightmare would be over. Jackie and Lee Peterson both thought their son was being set up, they said. Scott Peterson had been the only suspect in the eyes of the police since he had reported his pregnant wife missing on December 24, 2002, at 5:48 P.M. According to the Petersons, the police's objective from the beginning was to get Scott.

Jackie Peterson told us that their son was not a violent man and had never even been in a fight. She and Lee had their own perspective on the case and the investigation that had culminated in Scott's arrest.

At 5:17 P.M. on December 24, Peterson had phoned his mother-in-law, Sharon Rocha, with whom he and Laci were planning to spend Christmas Eve. He told her that McKenzie, the couple's golden retriever, was in the backyard, still wearing a leash, and Laci was not home. The last time that he'd seen his wife, she'd been inside the house preparing to walk the dog at about 9:30 A.M. At Sharon Rocha's suggestion, he called various friends in an attempt to locate Laci. Later he phoned Rocha back, saying that he had not been able to find her. He then began asking these friends to help search for Laci.

Detective Allen Brocchini arrived at the Peterson home just before 9:30 that night. He searched both Laci Peterson's Land Rover and Scott Peterson's Ford truck and later that night questioned Peterson extensively about his wife's disappearance.

By 10:00 P.M. it appeared that Brocchini was already convinced Peterson was responsible. Scott told his parents that at that time Brocchini cleared everyone out of the house, sat him down on the front porch, and said, "We know you did it. It's just a matter of time before we prove it."

It is well-established practice, if not actual policy, to immediately suspect the spouse in the homicide of a husband or wife. This conclusion is oftentimes correct, but not always. From the outset of their investigation, the Modesto police consistently interpreted all available facts to conform to their theory of Peterson's guilt. Seemingly, Detective Brocchini reached that conclusion on the night of December 24, before it was even known what had happened to Laci.

Later that night, Peterson allowed Brocchini to search his warehouse on North Emerald Avenue, and told him that there was no electricity in it. Using his vehicle's headlights and a flashlight, Brocchini searched the warehouse and the fourteen-foot boat inside it. The premises consisted of a warehouse and an adjoining office space sometimes referred to by Scott as a shop.

The day after Christmas, police served a search warrant on the warehouse and connecting office space. They found that there was indeed electricity—the inside office lights were working. They took this as proof that Peterson had lied to them, which reinforced Brocchini's belief in Scott's guilt.

Police wrote in a second search warrant affidavit that Scott told Brocchini that there were no lights in the shop. The implication is that Scott lied to him so that he could not see evidence hidden there. In reality, Brocchini was referring to the warehouse. True, Scott did not have lights in the warehouse. The adjoining space, where he had a desk, fax, and phone, had lights, and that's exactly what he said.

THE PHYSICAL EVIDENCE

Modesto police detectives Brocchini and Craig Grogan discovered a single strand of hair extending from a pair of pliers that was in Peterson's boat. Subsequent DNA testing showed that the hair could be Laci Peterson's. This was the only piece of physical evidence in the case against Peterson. No blood or tissue was found on the pliers, which were rusty and showed no signs of recent use.

The police theorized that Peterson killed his wife in their home, dragged her through the house on a throw rug, wrapped her in a tarp, put her into the back of his boat, and drove her to the San Francisco Bay, where he dumped her body. He then left what the police claim was a phony voice message on Laci's cell phone in which he addressed her as "beautiful" and asked her to pick up a Christmas gift at Vella Farms because he was running late and couldn't do it himself. Police also believed Peterson placed a leash on his and Laci's dog and released him into the neighborhood to divert suspicion.

The prosecution's theory requires acceptance of the fact that in carrying out this scheme, the only piece of physical evidence he left behind was a hair found in his boat, a hair that may or may not have been Laci's. Even if it was Laci's hair, there was an explanation for that. She visited the warehouse where the boat was kept three days before she disappeared. Scott told me he showed it to her, and a witness saw her at the warehouse.

After ten thousand hours of investigation over four months and as many as three hundred law enforcement personnel using every scientific aid to criminal investigation, they located a single strand of hair. This was the physical evidence against Scott Peterson.

In requesting another search warrant for the home and warehouse, Grogan wrote in a crime report: "Evidence at the scene suggested that Laci Peterson was the victim of a 'soft kill' where there would be limited blood evidence at the scene. The small amount of blood recovered in their bed could indicate a location where Laci Peterson had been assaulted."

The "small amount of blood" that Grogan refers to was more like a speck. The police suspicion at first seems understandable; however, at some point there must be a line drawn between suspicion and imagination.

Grogan continues: "The fact that Scott Peterson had no significant injuries aside from a scuffed knuckle indicates the victim did not likely have the ability to take defensive action. Laci may have been drugged prior to suffocation or poisoning, or otherwise incapacitated without a struggle. The cleanup by mopping the floor and vacuuming may be a result of wrapping Laci in a tarp outside the home and pulling her out the door, causing the throw rug to be wadded beneath the doorway. Scott could have carried Laci Peterson's body wrapped in a tarp to his vehicle and then transported her to his shop after releasing their dog with the leash attached."

He deduces all this from "evidence at the scene." Obviously, quite the contrary is true: There is no evidence to support a single one of the multiple conclusions he draws. There is no "evidence" at all, and yet Grogan is convinced that this is what happened. Other than traces of caffeine, no evidence of drugs or poison was ever detected in Laci's remains.

A far more reasonable analysis from a speck of blood, a pushed-up rug, and a dog on a leash would indicate that no homicide occurred on the premises, since nothing indicated that it had. Grogan's analysis can be supported only by a presumption of guilt.

MOTIVE

With Scott Peterson regarded as the prime suspect, the police sought a motive. Detective Grogan was told by Laci Peterson's mother, Sharon Rocha, and Rocha's longtime companion, Ron Grantski, that Laci wanted a large family, wanted to stop working as a substitute teacher, and wanted to stay at home with her children. She planned to buy a larger home and a new vehicle. Police wondered if her decisions had put too much financial pressure on Peterson and driven him to kill her.

But for a credible motive, they needed something more compelling than just Laci's possible plans for her home and family. On December 30, 2002, they thought they had it. After seeing Peterson's photograph in news stories about the case, Fresno-area massage therapist Amber Frey, twenty-seven, contacted Modesto police and told them that she'd been having an affair with him.

Working with police, Frey taped telephone calls from Peterson, who, when she confronted him about his wife, admitted that he had lied about his marital status but maintained his innocence in Laci's disappearance. Modesto police held a press conference on January 24, 2003, and Frey publicly revealed the affair.

In general, law enforcement tries to avoid press interviews

of prospective witnesses. However, the cooperation between the police and the media continued to be of significance in this case. The Amber Frey press conference was only the beginning.

On the same day as the Amber Frey conference, Laci's family, devastated by the news of Scott's affair, held a press conference of their own.

"I trusted him and stood by him in the initial phases of my sister's disappearance," said Laci's brother, Brent Rocha. "However, Scott has not been forthcoming with information regarding my sister's disappearance. I'm only left to question what else he may be hiding."

The press conferences enabled the police to commence a campaign of vilification against Scott by some of the media and eventually caused him seemingly irreparable damage.

Now Scott was seen in the court of public opinion as a cad, a philanderer, and a liar. To many observers, the emergence of Amber Frey provided what looked like a solid motive for murder.

I suspected that the police's belief of Scott's guilt had been further fueled by early television interviews Scott had granted to Gloria Gomez of the Sacramento CBS affiliate, KOVR, and Diane Sawyer of ABC's *Good Morning America.*

Peterson told Diane Sawyer on January 28, 2003, that he had never tried to hide his relationship with Amber Frey from police. "I told the police immediately," he said. He went on to say that he told them on Christmas Eve, the night Laci was reported missing. Although police were aware of the relationship as of December 30, Peterson did not actually admit to it until after the January 24 press conference where Amber Frey came forward.

In an interview with Gloria Gomez on January 29, he incorrectly stated that it was "shortly after Christmas Eve," that he told Amber Frey that he was married and his wife was missing. The wiretaps of Frey's phone reveal that he told her on January 6.

Since Peterson was trying to cover up his encounters with Frey, which was consistent with his previous actions, why did he subject himself to the questions he must have known he'd be asked by the television interviewers? That was one of the questions I asked the Petersons.

"Scott thought he could keep the story and the attention on Laci, and keep the public focused on finding Laci," Lee said. "He did the interviews thinking he could keep the story in the news, and it would help get information on her disappearance."

Unfortunately, the inconsistencies in the interviews only added to police suspicions that had begun the night Laci was reported missing.

THE ARREST

On April 13, 2003, the body of a male full-term fetus was discovered near Berkeley in the San Francisco Bay area. The next day, a woman walking her dog found a woman's body that had washed ashore near Point Isabel.

Dennis Rocha, Laci Peterson's father, told WBZ-TV in

Boston that he thought it would be only a matter of time before his son-in-law, Scott Peterson, was charged. Stanislaus County district attorney James Brazelton followed with a statement to the *Modesto Bee* that he felt "pretty strongly" that the body that had washed up was Laci Peterson's.

And finally, California attorney general Bill Lockyer called the case a "slam dunk." The attorney general is the chief law enforcement officer of the state. It is his office that will oppose Scott Peterson's appeal through the State Supreme Court. It is, of course, outrageous for a public official to publicly make such a prejudicial statement.

It was the Peterson family's belief that Scott was arrested on April 18 because authorities thought that he was fleeing the country to Mexico.

Lee Peterson said that on that day they were going to play golf in San Diego County, where he and his wife live. Lee showed us the starting sheet with his son's name on it. A starting sheet is prepared by the golf course "starter." This is the person who schedules the times people will start playing. Lee had reserved a time for himself and his sons, and the starter had prepared the sheet. "Scott was scheduled to play golf with me. He wasn't leaving the country," Lee said.

In fact, Scott was arrested in the parking lot of the golf course. At the time of his arrest, much was made of the fact that Scott was sporting freshly dyed blond hair. He was also carrying his brother's ID and nearly $15,000 in cash. Jackie explained that Scott was carrying his brother's ID that day in order to get a resident discount at the country club. The cash was proceeds from the sale of a car. A witness corroborates Scott tried to pay cash for a car near the time of his arrest.

Lee said Peterson's hair had been bleached in an attempt to help him dodge the media and the various extremists who were threatening to take his life.

"Ever since Laci disappeared, Scott has been a target everywhere he goes," Lee said.

He told us that somebody drove a truck through the front door of his son's office. If Peterson had been in the office, he could have been killed. As far as Lee and Jackie knew, the Modesto police had done nothing about it.

They also heard that a man with a criminal record had contacted Sharon Rocha, Laci's mother, offering to take out a contract on Peterson's life. Since the date of Laci's disappearance, the Peterson home had been burglarized twice, and apparently there was no police follow-up to those burglaries either.

Indeed, the Modesto police didn't seem to be concerned about Scott Peterson's safety. They allowed an outrageous radio personality to stand on his front lawn with a megaphone during a live broadcast, yelling "Murderer!" at the top of his lungs.

"Scott couldn't go home because this was occurring on his own property," Lee said. "He told us he no longer felt safe in Modesto."

Jackie then jumped in and said, "This will be straightened out when the police see that he was at his office using the computer and fax machine that morning when Laci disappeared."

I already guessed it wasn't going to be that easy to convince the police to let him go.

After listening to the Petersons' story, I said, "Even though they found the bodies, they're still continuing to drag the bay. From what I've heard, there is no actual physical evidence."

Without any solid evidence, the prosecution wasn't going to have much of a case. Police reported early in their investigation in a search warrant affidavit that they'd seen outlines of five cement anchors on the flatbed when they'd investigated Peterson's warehouse. We all knew that the search was on for these cement anchors that police suspected Scott had attached to Laci's limbs and head.

Although law enforcement would later discount this statement, investigators were still trying to prove that Scott had used cement to make five of these anchors, although only one was found in his boat. Peterson insisted that he made only one anchor but was not certain of the exact date. He thought it was the Thursday, Friday, or Saturday prior to Laci's disappearance. He told police that he made only one anchor and then poured the leftover cement powder in the dirt near the top of his driveway. He said the same thing during a wiretapped phone call to Laci's brother, Brent Rocha. He produced a receipt from Home Depot showing he had spent less than $5 on a small bag of cement.

(Later, when we saw the photograph of the supposed outlines on the flatbed, Geragos and I started laughing as we compared it to the statement in the search warrant affidavit. Indeed, it was dropped from future warrants.)

Lee pointed out that Scott had been raised around boats from the time he was three years old.

"My family has had a lot of boats," Lee said. "These small cement anchors are used all the time."

He continued venting about the police and the anchor. "They think he dumped Laci in the bay," he said. "They think this because they found a cement anchor. How dumb. Doesn't anyone in the Modesto Police Department own a boat? Doesn't anyone know that cement anchors are made all the time by people who don't want to spend two hundred dollars on an anchor? Now they run crazy with this idea that he drowned Laci using an anchor. They're out to get my son."

Police hoped to find more evidence in the mop bucket they found at the Peterson home. Jon Evers, the first police officer to appear at the house that night, spotted a mop and bucket sitting outside near a door. Scott told police that Laci was getting ready to mop the entryway floor when he left between 9:30 and 9:45 the morning of December 24.

Detective Brocchini asked to have the mop and bucket removed and tested. Police didn't think Laci Peterson would have mopped her floor the day after the maid had been there, and concluded that Peterson must have mopped it. That's all the tabloids needed. They incorrectly reported that blood and vomit matching Laci's DNA were found on the mop; they said that the house reeked of bleach on the night of the twenty-fourth. All of this was pure tabloid fantasy.

Jackie and Lee said that their son had told them he hadn't gone near the bleach. It was another false story. The presumption of guilt seemed to pervade each development in the case.

A SECOND PREGNANT WOMAN

Near the end of our initial meeting, Jackie proceeded to tell us a possible theory about what might have happened to Laci: A deputy district attorney from a nearby county had been threatened by gang members, Jackie told us. The woman, who lived in the same neighborhood as Scott and Laci, was also in the late stage of pregnancy. Furthermore, she also had a golden retriever, and as was the case with Scott and Laci, her dog's name was McKenzie. I later confirmed these facts in police reports.

That theory resonated with me. It wasn't that far of a stretch that a gang-related revenge killing could have targeted Laci by mistake. I told the Petersons that when I was working as a gang prosecutor in Compton, California, my life had been threatened more than once. At the very least, their theory was believable and a very, very strange coincidence. It was the first of many strange coincidences that I would encounter and the first of several alternate theories about what might have happened to Laci Peterson.

It appeared to me that the police had responded to the considerable public pressure they felt to resolve the case, and that they had focused only on Scott Peterson and convinced themselves of his guilt. Thereafter, it seemed that they had taken an adversarial position to any facts or theories inconsistent with their beliefs.

I got the impression that the Petersons had no idea how the media, and thus the public, were reacting to this case. Jackie, Lee, and apparently Scott thought it was going to be straightened out. They trusted Mark Geragos—and by association, me—to make it right.

I think it's fair to describe Mark Geragos as a man who always appears to be in a hurry—probably because he is. Meetings with Mark are difficult to schedule and even more difficult to execute. His schedule is busy.

Geragos excused himself at one point during the meeting on this Saturday. After he left the room momentarily, Lee turned to me. "Matt," he said softly, "tell me everything's going to be all right."

"Well, you've got one of the best trial lawyers in the state on your side," I replied, trying to give Lee whatever comfort I could.

I believed what I told him. I saw no reason why everything couldn't be all right.

2

ATTORNEY FOR THE ACCUSED

We officially took over Scott Peterson's defense on May 2. Local Modesto lawyer Kirk McAllister, originally hired by Scott in the weeks immediately following Laci's disappearance, remained a part of the defense team through the preliminary hearing in October 2003.

A few days after meeting with the Petersons, Mark Geragos and I flew from Los Angeles to Modesto with investigator Bill Pavelic. A former captain with the Los Angeles Police Department, Pavelic is a big, likable man with a thick Polish accent. He's also a very smart investigator, with good common sense.

Years of running a burglary detail taught him how important it is to get his facts not from textbooks but from flesh-and-blood informants. Pavelic was a very good street cop who knew how to talk to people, and that proved to be extremely helpful in our investigation.

Upon arriving in Modesto, the three of us went to the public defender's office, where we picked up about one thousand pages of discovery—that is, the facts of the investigation. *Discovery* is a legal term that describes the process of gathering information from the prosecution in preparation for trial. The purpose of doing discovery, according to the law, is to promote the ascertainment of truth in trials. Under California law the prosecution was required to give us all relevant evidence seized or obtained as a part of their investigation. Obviously, the one thousand pages wasn't all they had on the case, but the prosecution was giving us the discovery in small increments. No explanation was ever given as to why this was being done, and it continued to be an apparent strategy throughout the pretrial phase of the case.

The one thousand or so pages we did manage to get that day consisted of newspaper articles about the case and transcripts from television shows, including *Larry King Live,* even one where King is interviewing Mark Geragos. It also contained reports regarding psychics and one mystic who had attempted to locate the bodies with a divining rod. Mixed in with all of that, we found what appeared to be some relevant documents. Although we were eager to continue looking through the discovery, Mark went to see Scott in the Stanislaus County jail while Pavelic and I visited Scott's warehouse.

While we were at the warehouse, a witness who worked in

the same complex approached us and volunteered the information that Laci had been there a few days before her disappearance. Laci, the witness said, asked to use the witness's bathroom because Scott had his work products stacked all over his warehouse, and it was difficult to get to the bathroom there. The witness said that she told the police what she told us, yet a report was never provided to us.

This information would prove crucial later in the case when the prosecution maintained that Laci had never visited Scott's warehouse and didn't know about his boat.

Pavelic and I had arranged next to meet Lee and Jackie at Scott and Laci's house. We stopped at a gas station to buy a map of Modesto. Out of curiosity, I asked the attendant if she could tell us where to find the Peterson house. She gave me directions and added, "I get asked that a lot. You're about the fifth person who's asked me today."

We followed her directions but found that we couldn't get close to the house. Our way was blocked by the numbers of people gawking at the house. Many were leaving cards and flowers outside. Lee and Jackie met us. They had to park a block away. We decided not to go inside; instead, we would return another time.

Mark met up with us after his visit to Scott in jail. He didn't say much about the meeting. He just handed me a form and said, "Fill this out. This is to get your jail pass. You are going to be spending a lot of time in there with him."

The flight back to L.A. took our tiny plane through heavy turbulence. Even as we were being violently bounced around in the air, we were eager to examine the discovery documents we had received. We were able to locate significant areas of interest as we quickly read through the material.

One intriguing report involved a gold Croton watch like one owned by Laci that was missing. The watch in the report had been pawned at a Modesto pawn shop close to her house shortly after her disappearance.

Another report confirmed that the mop in the bucket on the Peterson side porch tested negative for blood, negative for vomit, negative for any physical evidence. These reports were looking encouraging.

On that upbeat note, we decided that I would return to Modesto to live there and work closely with Scott Peterson and begin the investigation of the case. The first step would be for me to meet our client.

In taking on Scott Peterson's defense, we never deluded ourselves into thinking that the case had no problems. We could not ignore the presence of some suspicious circumstances, such as Scott's fishing trip ninety miles away in the same area where the bodies were found. We did think, however, that although the case had suspicion, it was awfully short on proof and that far too much of the prosecution's case was based solely on speculation without sufficient facts to support a finding of guilt.

After arriving home in Los Angeles after our rocky flight, I turned right around and drove back to Modesto. I booked a room at the Doubletree Hotel, where I spent the rest of the evening reading more of the discovery. About 7:00 the next morning, I went to meet Scott Peterson.

I reported in at the jail and was put into the lineup room, a dingy, windowless room with cinder-block walls, two chairs, a table, and a large one-way glass mirror. This is where almost all of our meetings ended up taking place. I spent about one hundred hours in this police lineup room talking to Scott Peterson. Sitting in there we could see our reflections in the one-way mirror but couldn't tell if anyone was on the other side.

Police use the lineup-room procedure so witnesses can anonymously observe potential suspects. A witness identification or misidentification at a live lineup can be a very powerful piece of evidence at trial. Lineup rooms, from my experience, are used by law enforcement for that purpose only. I had never heard of them being used for attorney-client meetings.

Two deputies brought in Peterson. He hobbled inside wearing an orange jumpsuit, his hands and feet in shackles. His face was puffy, as if he hadn't slept at all, and his bleached hair stood on end. He reached out both of his hands to shake mine.

I introduced myself and told him, "I'm moving to Modesto. I'm going to be seeing you every day while I investigate this case for the defense. Are they treating you okay?"

He seemed like a kid totally out of place, out of his environment. He told me he felt his arrest was a misunderstanding and was confident it would be straightened out.

He had been doing yoga on the floor of his cell to help alleviate the stress, he said. He'd been assigned to his own cell, next to an inmate who, because of his seniority, was in charge of the TV remote for the high-security block where Peterson was housed. The inmate had protected Peterson when another inmate began harassing him, yelling that Peterson was a wife and baby killer.

He was permitted to spend one hour a week outside in the yard with other high-security inmates. When he went out there, two deputies watched him, and he had to keep his shackles on. In fact, any time he was taken out of his cell, they kept him in shackles.

He told me he was spending a lot of his jail time in the law library. I suggested that he read *Sheppard v. Maxwell,* a 1966 U.S. Supreme Court case regarding prejudicial news coverage. Osteopath Dr. Sam Sheppard had been convicted in 1954 of the murder of his pregnant wife. Massive publicity surrounded the case, including allegations of extramarital affairs. The Supreme Court reversed Sheppard's conviction on the grounds that pretrial prejudice and adverse media exposure denied him due process of law.

A second jury acquitted him in less than twelve hours of deliberation. With the case of Scott Peterson, the appeals process will again have to deal with the issue of a defendant being tried simultaneously in the court and the press.

As I talked more to Scott over the following weeks and months, I again got the feeling I'd had when I first met him— that he was docile. He certainly didn't seem to fit the profile of a psychopath, and he didn't strike me as a killer. I couldn't imagine this young man doing anything like what he'd been accused of. I remembered what Jackie said when we met with her and Lee: "Scott is nonviolent. He's just like me."

I was careful what I said in that first and all subsequent meetings. To observe an attorney and client is not illegal; to listen to their conversation is. A contact of mine from Modesto warned me, "They're listening to you. I know because when I was a jailer there several years ago, we used to listen."

I also knew that telephone conversations between Scott and his Modesto criminal attorney, Kirk McAllister, had been intercepted by the police. Wiretapping is a very important tool used by law enforcement (after establishing a sufficient reason and securing a court order) to legally listen in on telephone calls involving someone they suspect of a crime. After Laci disappeared, the police began listening in on all of Peterson's phone calls made from home. Conversations between him and his mother, his father, Amber Frey, and his lawyer were all secretly recorded.

The prosecution was required by law to provide this information to the defense. During my investigation, I listened to most of these recordings. In these conversations, Peterson never confessed or admitted to anything incriminating.

The police were especially interested when Peterson retained the services of Kirk McAllister. On January 20, 2003, Detective Grogan wrote a report about a wiretapped telephone conversation between Peterson and his father. "On January 20, 2003, at 1258 hours, Scott calls his father ("Chief"). Scott tells his father that this was a 'no bail case since it is capital.' Scott said it was comforting to talk with McAllister."

Grogan concluded in his report: "I'm still asking myself why a husband of a missing person would be concerned with the bail schedule on a murder-charge booking. I'm also wondering what's so comforting with talking to Kirk McAllister when your pregnant wife has yet to be found." Grogan did not understand that Peterson never asked his lawyer about bail.

Conversations between an attorney and his client are privileged. Police are not allowed to listen in on those conversations. Even though that is a firmly established, well-known rule of law, it was violated by law enforcement during the Peterson investigation.

Kirk McAllister was a former Modesto deputy district attorney who in the past had worked closely with the investigators in charge of wiretapping Peterson. They knew McAllister, knew his voice. Yet the police were so zealous in their investigation that they taped Peterson and McAllister anyway.

Peterson made several phone calls to McAllister because he wanted the lawyer to intercede to help him get his computer and other personal property back from the police. The police monitored some of these calls. One phone call between McAllister and Peterson starts off with Peterson identifying the person to whom he is speaking by saying, "Hello, Kirk." Even so, police continued to listen for the next minute and twenty-eight seconds as Peterson and his lawyer discussed his case. This was another example of the aggressive investigative strategy the police were using to make a case against Peterson.

From the start, I was extremely cautious in my meetings

with Scott. We often communicated by passing notes back and forth, which made interviewing him very difficult.

While in the lineup room with its one-way glass, I was convinced that we were under constant observation. I tested my theory on one visit by pretending to pass something to Peterson under the table. When he walked out after my visit, they strip-searched him and continued to do so every time I visited. They also checked my briefcase before every visit after that, although they never had before. This seemed to confirm that we were being watched. I can only speculate that they were also listening, but I have no way of knowing for sure.

In California the prosecution in felony cases is required by law to present evidence to a neutral magistrate at a preliminary hearing. The magistrate is then to make a finding as to whether there exists probable cause that the suspect has committed the crime. In the Peterson case, they were required to do this within ten days of Scott's pleading not guilty to the charges. Scott very reluctantly waived his right to have the preliminary hearing within ten days. He even expressed his reluctance on the record, stating, in essence, that he felt he had no choice because the prosecution was not giving us all the discovery material. We couldn't prepare for the hearing if we didn't know the facts that made up their case.

The day we met, I was to pick up several thousand more pages of discovery. This was a big moment for both of us. I promised Scott that I would start reading it immediately and let him know anything I found out. He was eager to hear what I learned and seemed absolutely certain about the outcome. I left that first meeting with him determined to find something that may have been overlooked in this case.

After leaving Scott, I went to the district attorney's office and picked up the five thousand additional pages of discovery. By the time I left the case, more than thirty thousand of the forty thousand pages of discovery had been given to the defense. The prosecution trickled the documents to us in small increments, usually a couple thousand pages at a time. In fact, they were still handing documents over to the defense even after the trial started.

The prosecution had told us that the crux of its case was in the first six thousand pages. Having fueled myself with coffee, I headed back to the Doubletree and began what would be two straight days of reading.

Beginning at page five thousand and continuing in reverse numerical order, I delved into the reports, interviews, and dispatch logs relating to Laci Peterson's disappearance. It was clear from reading through the material that the police had been expending a lot of effort trying to find Laci. Their other focus, of course, was Scott Peterson. There was no specific order to any of the information. It contained miscellaneous newspaper articles, reports of Laci sightings, transcripts from television shows on the subject, as well as expert reports on Scott's facial expressions and what they meant. Scattered among all of that was the prosecution's actual case.

The district attorney's office had numbered all of the pages, starting at page one. They let us work with it long enough so that we could practically commit the page numbers to memory, then gave us a second set of discovery, which included what was in the first set as well as new material—all with new page numbers. Thus, we had two sets of the same reports with different numbers on them. This made it difficult for us to reference the documents that were given to us.

They seemed to be complying with the requirement of the law without making it particularly easy for us. Nevertheless, as I reviewed the materials, I continued to believe that this case could be defended successfully.

DOCUMENT 4560

The newly acquired discovery contained some startling information that had never been reported publicly. One of the first items to grab my attention was a police report dated December 30, 2002. In the report, Officer Tyler of the Modesto police wrote:

> *On 12-28-02 I received information from a Sexual Assault Counselor, and stated that approximately two weeks ago she helped a confidential victim of sexual assault. The counselor stated that during the interview of the victim the victim stated that she was lured into a brown van (Chevy or Ford) by her ex-girlfriend. While in the van two men and two women raped the victim and a satanic ritual was conducted. The victim told the*

counselor that the group frequents area parks and was currently living at Woodward Reservoir. The counselor stated the victim said that during the ritual the group mentioned a Christmas Day Death and that she would read about it in the paper.

After hearing about Laci's disappearance, the counselor was concerned enough to inform Officer Tyler, who was also her brother-in-law. Such reports to counselors protect the victims' identities, so we were unable to locate the woman. But the victim had told the counselor the name of one of those involved, and the officer located four people in a brown van, living in the Woodward Reservoir. The group turned out to be a family. The parents, Antoine and Peggy W——,* lived there with their adult son and daughter, Tom and Karen. Tom had been charged and convicted of cruelty to animals a few years before. They were from the airport district of Modesto, now living at different campsites. The airport district refers to a low-income neighborhood near the Modesto airport that borders the Petersons' neighborhood.

When this family was interviewed by police, they were not arrested. They did admit to the officer that they had been near Laci's neighborhood around Christmas and had noticed that Yosemite Boulevard was blocked off with police vehicles. They said the reason for the visit was to get parts for their brown van.

---

* When a dash follows the first appearance of a name, that name has been changed to protect the identity of the individual.

The story struck me as suspicious. They claimed that they drove twenty-five miles from where they were camping, past more than a dozen auto-parts stores, to get parts for their van?

This group had been accused of abducting a woman, and according to the victim, they promised they would be back to do it again, around Christmastime. But this time it was not going to be a rape, but a murder.

Still, no arrests were made. The police apparently did not feel it was worth pursuing, and ultimately, I heard that the rape counselor was fired for disclosing the information.

WITNESSES IN THE NEIGHBORHOOD

A separate police report revealed that on the night of December 23, a neighbor of Laci and Scott's, Simon L——, was sitting in his car in front of his house listening to a police scanner. He observed what he thought was a suspicious-looking brown van followed by two cars. Simon L—— followed the van down Encina Avenue in the direction of the Peterson house. Two people got out of the van and approached his car. He accelerated around them and sped off. This occurred two short blocks from Laci's house the night of December 23.

The first two times Simon L—— called to report this to police, he was ignored. One of the police dispatch logs reflects that he was angry about the lack of response. Finally, police detectives Trogdon and Ray Bennett met with Simon L—— at the

Modesto Police Department on January 23, 2003, and took the following statement:

> Simon L—— stated that on 12-23-02 at approximately 2100–2130 hours he was sitting in his car in front of his residence. Simon L—— said he was sitting in his car listening to his scanner and watching for burglars. Simon L—— stated as he was sitting in his car he noticed a 1985 to 1995 brown cargo five window van with tinted windows. Simon L—— said the van did not have any doors on the sides, but did have some to the rear. Simon L—— also described the van as "extra heavy, like a 3/4 ton." Simon L—— stated the van drove by his residence and it was being followed by a white, 4 door car, which looked like a Honda, but it was not a Honda.
>
> Simon L—— stated that the van and white car drove by his residence two other times, so he became suspicious and decided to follow them. Simon L—— said the vehicles drove down to the end of his street and then turned left, heading westbound on Encina. Simon L—— stated he drove down his street and decided to turn down Roble, which is one street before Encina. Simon L—— told me that when he turned westbound on Roble, he saw that the van was now stopped on Roble, facing eastbound. Simon L—— said as he got closer to the van, a white male adult, clean cut, 6'0, 200–230 lbs, 35–40 years old, short to medium length dark brown or black hair, receding in the front, wearing a tan hunting jacket

and jeans got out of the driver's seat and attempted to stop him. Simon L—— stated this male was not wearing any kind of identification as a police officer, so he decided to drive around the subject.

Simon L—— told me as he drove by the van, he noticed two other people near the back doors of the van. Simon L—— said he also saw the white, Honda looking car stopped at the stop sign on Covena at Roble facing southbound. Simon L—— stated there was also another white car, which reminded him of a Lexus stopped behind the white Honda looking vehicle. Simon L—— stated one of the subjects from the van flagged the cars over, at which time both white cars turned eastbound on Roble in front of him. Simon L—— said he had to swerve to avoid hitting the second white car. Simon L—— stated the van and the two cars then left eastbound on Roble until they got to Rosina where they turned left heading northbound. The van and two cars then turned eastbound on Encina and then turned northbound on Seagull Way, where Simon L—— said he stopped watching them.

In this statement, Simon L—— described for police a vehicle that could have been the same brown van that had been involved in the reported satanic rape and abduction that took place two weeks before Laci disappeared. And now it appears it may have been just two blocks from where Laci would disappear the following day.

• • •

Police logs indicate that at about 11:30 A.M. on December 24, the morning Laci was last seen, neighbor Diane Jackson saw a house being burglarized across the street from the Petersons' home. Jackson described watching the burglars load a safe into the back of a brown van. She later made a tentative identification of the brown van this group at the Woodward Reservoir was driving, saying that from behind, "It could be the same van I saw across from the Petersons' the morning of the twenty-fourth."

I called Geragos at once. We were both extremely excited and encouraged by these developments.

"The people in the brown van at the Woodward Reservoir admitted that they were in the neighborhood around the time of Laci's disappearance," I said. "And we have witnesses who independently reported seeing a similar brown van in the neighborhood the night of the twenty-third and morning of the twenty-fourth. And it appears they may have lied to police about their reasons for being there."

There were no other reports about the people in the brown van staying at the reservoir. The paragraph-long police report taken by the counselor's brother-in-law was all the information we had on the group. I needed to learn more about them, about the earlier abduction, and about the burglary across the street from the Petersons' on the morning that Laci disappeared. First and foremost, I needed to find Antoine and Peggy W——, their adult children, Tom and Karen, and their brown van.

The park ranger at the Woodward Reservoir recalled having seen them hanging around the campsite with another group, camping next to each other. The two groups had gotten into an argument around Christmas and left the park at the same time, he said.

The rape victim reported that one of her attackers mentioned a Christmas Day death. Somebody in this group may have known something, but incredibly there was no information in the documents I had before me indicating that the police had followed up on them. The police report I reviewed was marked "NFA," which I believe means no further action.

I went to see Scott and told him what I had found out. He wanted us to bring all of this new evidence to the attention of the judge as soon as possible. Needless to say, he wanted out of jail.

I then met Lee and Jackie Peterson at the Doubletree. I'd made a diagram of Scott and Laci's neighborhood showing the suspicious activity occurring around the time of Laci's disappearance. I spread it out in the lobby, but before I could explain what I'd learned, I realized that someone in the lobby was aiming a television camera at us.

This was the way the Petersons lived, with media following them everywhere they went. This was my first encounter with media in Modesto, and I was so focused on what I had discovered that I didn't really pay attention to the camera.

"Come on," Lee said. "We shouldn't have met here. It's full of press."

We got up immediately and were on our way out of the hotel when the manager escorted us to a private conference room. I spread out the map and described to them all the criminal activity in the neighborhood. I told them that a police report existed about a satanic group in a brown van that was involved in abducting and raping a young woman about two weeks before Laci disappeared. The group said there would be a Christmas Day death. There were witnesses in the neighborhood who called the police describing a brown van in Laci's neighborhood the night of the twenty-third and the morning of the twenty-fourth. The witnesses appeared to be describing the same brown van, I said.

In addition, I told them, according to the police report, the group admitted they were in the area of Laci's neighborhood around Christmas; however, they claimed that they were getting parts for their van, twenty-five miles from their campsite. From what I had seen, the police did not seem to put any pressure on them with their questioning, I told the Petersons.

In one of the search warrant affidavits prepared by the police, they reported "three witnesses who saw a brown van" in the neighborhood around the time of Laci's disappearance. I had found two of those witnesses in the discovery and also told the Petersons about them.

Jackie had tears in her eyes, and Lee was looking at the ground, speechless, his face red.

Jackie hugged me. "Oh, my God," she said. "Our family's followed up on every lead for more than five months since Laci disappeared, and no one ever told us about this."

"And the police know about it?" Lee asked angrily.

"Yes," I said.

"Have the police or anyone done anything about it?" Lee asked, astonished.

"It doesn't appear that they did anything," I told him.

We couldn't talk much longer because Jackie and Lee had to leave so they would be on time for their scheduled meeting with their son. They were allowed to see him for two half-hour visits per week. They drove from San Diego County each week for these visits. The routine was to see Scott for a half hour on Thursday and a half hour on Friday. I would meet with them on one of the days, usually at a restaurant, and we would go over the status of my investigation.

"Don't stay here anymore," Lee advised me as we got ready to leave. "It's full of press. We always stay at the Red Lion on the outskirts of town."

I assured him that I'd do the same next time. The Petersons and I were exuberant as we discussed what I had found out and what I was going to do next.

"Follow up," I said. "We've got to find those people."

From the Modesto police report, I obtained the license number of the brown van driven by the family who had been camping at the Woodward Reservoir. It was registered to the owner of an auto body shop in Ceres, a small city just south of Modesto off highway 99. As soon as I said good-bye to the Petersons, I drove there.

The shop owner told me he had sold the 1987 van to a Peggy W——, the same name contained in Officer Tyler's report about the abduction and rape. She had given him a cash down payment, but after the van was driven off, he never received another payment or saw Peggy or her family again. However, the shop owner knew the whole bunch, since at one time they had lived just across the street.

"I heard they ran out on their rent payment, too," he said. "They lived right over there." He pointed to a one-story apartment unit across the dirt road from where we were standing.

"They were a dangerous group," he recalled. "You can talk to this guy if you want to know more about them," he said, handing me a piece of paper on which he'd written a telephone number. "His name is Billy ——, and he used to be married to their daughter. He can tell you all about that bunch. He ran with them for a while until he got fed up with them."

The shop owner said that Billy, Karen's ex-husband, was a good man who didn't belong with the group. "For one thing, he's honest," he said.

"Where does Billy live?" I asked.

"I'm not sure where he's staying anymore, but he might still be out by the airport."

I thanked the man and left. Then I walked over to the W—— family's former apartment and tried to talk to some rough-looking characters who were hanging around outside. I asked if they knew the family or had seen their brown van around lately. At first they didn't answer. Finally one said they had left around Christmastime, and he hadn't seen them since. He wouldn't give me his name.

I was able to locate Karen's ex-husband, Billy, who lived in the airport district of Modesto. He was very cooperative, possibly because of his low opinion of his former in-laws. He told me that the family members were drug users, had guns, and moved from one campsite to another in their brown van.

Since I was getting nowhere trying to find them, I decided I might have better luck trying to find the van itself. I bought the title to it for two hundred dollars from the shop owner and hired three companies to try to repossess it. They were to be paid only upon making a recovery.

We searched every campsite from Woodward Reservoir to Sacramento looking for this group in the brown van. Mark Geragos held a press conference and asked the public's help in trying to locate the woman who had reported being abducted and raped by a satanic group. What I had hoped would be a private investigation suddenly turned into a contest between the police and us to see who would find the van first. The police won.

Why were they suddenly so interested in recovering the brown van?

One afternoon soon thereafter, Mark called me and announced, "They found your van."

I was frustrated and didn't do a very good job of hiding the fact. The police wanted Scott Peterson, period. At this point, I was convinced of it. I had little confidence that they would explore any evidence in the van that might actually point toward a different theory of the crime.

The police held on to the van for more than a month. It was a painfully long time. As the days went by without any news, I was concerned that if they found something helpful to the defense, it probably wouldn't be developed and more than likely would be deflected.

When the police finally notified me that I could come claim the van, investigator Bill Pavelic and I went to pick it up at the Modesto Police Department. Inside, there was gray duct tape, black electrical tape, red and black candles, and more than ten spots that looked like bloodstains. The apparent bloodstains had been circled with blue ink. I asked the police if they'd tested them, and they said no.

At trial it was learned that the Modesto Police Department did in fact test the blood found in the brown van. It was determined by the police that none of the stains were human blood. The defense never conducted its own testing.

All of these items could have been relevant to the investigation, but the police didn't seem interested, and we lacked the resources to do any more, since that would have required a team of equipped crime-scene investigators.

We also discovered eight car batteries in the van. Pavelic asked the police if they'd written stolen property reports regarding the batteries and whether they were conducting an investigation into the group that reportedly committed the abduction and rape just before Laci disappeared. As usual, their answer was no.

THE CROTON WATCH

During the time that I was trying to locate the W. family and their brown van, I was also following up on the intriguing item in the discovery about the gold Croton watch that had been pawned on December 31.

The police had gone through all of Laci's clothes and jewelry to determine what she was wearing when she disappeared. They were unable to find the gold Croton watch that, according to Scott Peterson, she had put on that morning. Nor could they find the earrings that Scott said she had worn the last time he saw her. Police found Laci's Croton watch case, which was open and empty, on her dresser.

Close to Laci's house, on December 31, a woman pawned a yellow gold Croton woman's watch. This appeared to match the description of Laci's missing Croton watch. We got this information from a copy of the pawn ticket in the discovery. There was no police report connected to it, just the pawn ticket. Convinced that we might have located Laci's missing watch, I made numerous attempts to get it.

The pawnshop, which was ten minutes from Laci's house, smelled like old furniture. Consisting of two adjoining rooms of wall-to-wall merchandise, it had the usual array of jewelry and watches. Every bit of space in the store had been utilized—even the ceiling, where musical instruments were hung.

The pawnbroker wouldn't even come out of the back to talk to me. I wrote him a note, telling him that I'd pay him $300 for the watch. Based on the information on the pawn ticket, I believed that he'd paid around $25, so I was offering him a $275 profit. He wouldn't respond to my offer.

On subsequent visits, when I attempted to get information from him, he referred me to the Modesto police.

Laci had inherited the watch, and Scott and Laci had been attempting to sell it on eBay. A videotape showing the watch, presumably made for insurance purposes, was part of a video that was about forty minutes long. A hand that appears to be Laci's arranges jewelry on a black cloth: a Mickey Mouse watch, some necklaces, a pair of earrings, and the Croton watch.

A description of the video appeared in a police report included in the discovery:

> When viewing this video found in Scott and Laci PE-
> TERSON's video camera, I saw the first images on the
> tape were of Laci PETERSON and Stacey BOYERS.
> The person filming appeared to be Scott PETERSON
> based on his voice being heard on the audio portion of
> the film. Laci and Stacey were wearing bikini tops and
> the photographs appeared to have been taken during
> the summer time. Laci was cooking something in the
> kitchen while Scott videoed her and Stacey. [. . .]
>
> On the same tape there was a video of someone mix-
> ing chemicals. It appeared to be related to Scott PETER-
> SON's work.
>
> Also in the video were images of Lee PETERSON, Joe
> PETERSON and what appeared to be some teenage

boys fishing in a mountainous area. Scott was again op-
erating the video as his voice could be heard coming
from the area of the filming.

Also there were images of Scott and Laci PETER-
SON's swimming pool and the watches and jewelry that
I recognized had been listed on Ebay. It appeared that
both Scott and Laci were involved in filming or the at-
tempted sale of the jewelry as Laci's voice could be
heard on the video and both Scott and Laci's hands were
visible moving the jewelry around. The images from the
video were apparently used for the Ebay photographs of
that jewelry. In the images of the jewelry was the Croton
gold and diamond watch, which was at this point in the
investigation unaccounted for.

Modesto police detective Craig Grogan watched the video, and
during the two minutes he viewed it, the watch hand didn't
move. Based on that, he concluded that Laci wouldn't have
been wearing it because it wasn't working. It appeared from the
discovery that the investigation ended there.

By physically examining the watch, we would have been
able to tell if it was, in fact, Laci's. It seemed that the police had
no interest in following up on it. I felt that it was one of the most
important pieces of evidence leading us to the possible killer or
killers in the case, and the police wouldn't let us near it. The police could have quickly obtained this information. The pawnshop business is heavily regulated, since it is an obvious conduit
for stolen property.

If this watch had turned out to be Laci's, it might have led to critical evidence, taking the investigation in an entirely different direction. This was one of many areas where I attempted to properly investigate what I believe the police should have been doing in the first place, but I was shut down and denied by the pawnbroker's lack of cooperation.

The idea that Laci was wearing a gold Croton watch when she disappeared and one was pawned a few blocks away soon after her disappearance was suspicious enough, but the situation got even more suspicious.

As I studied the pawn slip, I realized that the woman who pawned the watch had an almost identical last name to the family connected to the brown van staying at the Woodward Reservoir. Although both names were pronounced the same, one ended in a *w* and the other with an *e*.

I followed up on that lead as well as I could but was unable to locate the woman who had pawned the watch or to determine if she had any relationship to the people in the van. I don't know if the police have ever tried to locate her. With their resources, she could have easily been located and questioned.

The earlier excitement and optimism I had felt on the plane ride from Modesto was turning into an overwhelming sense of frustration. We had information regarding a rape and abduction two weeks before Laci's disappearance, and a boast that there was to be a Christmas Day death. The victim claimed all of this took place in a brown van. The police had been told where the group in the van was staying. A witness had described a brown van in Laci's neighborhood the night before her disappearance, and another witness had described a brown van involved in a burglary at 11:30 A.M. on December 24, the morning of Laci's disappearance, literally across the street from the Peterson residence.

A gold watch that we believed could have belonged to Laci had been pawned within a week following her disappearance. The last name signed by the person pawning the watch was almost the same as the people in the brown van staying at the Woodward Reservoir.

Just six months earlier, as a deputy district attorney, I could have quickly and easily pursued these seemingly incriminating circumstances. However, things were different now. Nobody is required to talk to the lawyer or investigator for an accused murderer.

The defense had limited funds, no subpoena power for investigations, no way to offer benefits or immunity for cooperating witnesses, no unlimited access to documents, and very little, if any, cooperation from public agencies and prosecution witnesses.

I was feeling a sense of helplessness and frustration that I had never experienced when I was a deputy district attorney.

3

CRIMES IN THE NEIGHBORHOOD

The day Laci Peterson disappeared was not a typical peaceful Christmas Eve in her Modesto neighborhood. Although the unusual amount of crime and strange behavior in the neighborhood that day was not well known, I found several phone calls had been made to the Modesto Police Department reporting crimes and possible crimes occurring right around the time Laci disappeared. The only reason I can assume that it wasn't well publicized is because of the police's focus on proving Scott Peterson guilty.

SUSPICIOUS NIGHTTIME ACTIVITY IN
LACI'S NEIGHBORHOOD

Several "door-knock" incidents were reported on the night of December 23. Judge Ricardo Cordova on Edgebrook, a block away from the Petersons, was wakened that evening. A man came to his door with a story of woe and asked for money. Suspecting he was casing the neighborhood, Cordova refused to give him any money.

The same night, Brenna and Mike Buhler, who lived on Severin Avenue, two blocks from Laci's house, also responded to a knock on their door by a strange man.

He claimed to be a neighbor from down the street. The man said that his wife, who was a nurse at Tuolumne General Hospital, had her car break down and had their only credit card. He asked if the Buhlers would loan him some money for gas so that he could get to her. Brenna gave him a couple of dollars, and her husband, thinking he would need more, gave him $15, then began to have a "funny feeling" about him, he said.

To get the $17 back, he told the man that he could give him a $20 in exchange for it. The man gave it back. At that time Buhler asked him what his address was.

The subject answered with a number that Buhler knew did not exist. He asked the man to show him where he lived, and they began walking. They passed a Chevy pickup with a driver inside. Buhler asked about it, and the man said it was his uncle, who was waiting for him. Was this person casing houses? The

Buhlers thought the conduct was suspicious enough to call the police.

There was another reported incident five blocks from the Peterson house involving Helen V——. That report stated:

Helen V—— said that . . . at about 1730 there was a knock on the door. A subject was there stating that he lived around the corner and needed some money. Although Helen V—— knew that he did not live right around the corner, she felt that he might live in some apartments a couple of blocks away. The man went on to say that his wife was broken down in Greely Hill, had the ATM card, credit card, and all the cash. Therefore he was asking to borrow $30 so that he could fill up his tank and go get her. The man said that he would return in about three hours with the money and some wine.

Since Helen V—— only had a $50 bill, she gave that to him. At about midnight, as Helen V—— was getting ready for bed, the man returned. He said he was there to repay her and flashed some money that he was holding, however Helen V—— could not see how much it was. The man claimed that he only had a $100 bill and needed some change. Helen V—— told him that she did not have any change but that her mother, who had already gone to bed, might have. Helen V—— told the man to give her the $100 bill, and she would go see if her mother had the change. He told Helen V—— that he *would hold the $100 and for her to go see if her mother had the change and then come back. He wanted or acted as if he wanted to come into the house, however, Helen V—— told him to wait on the porch.*

He was also claiming that he had brought some wine and was yelling around the corner to "Judy" to bring the wine to the house.

Helen V——'s mother, Christine, had a $50 bill. When Helen V—— went back to the doorway and was holding the $50 bill in her hand, the man reached into the residence and took the $50 out of her hand. The man then ran eastbound on Julian to Fusco, southbound on Fusco, where he got onto a bike that was around the corner, and was last seen riding his bike eastbound on Roland.

[The officer] went over the part where the man reached out and grabbed the $50 bill very carefully with Helen V—— and actually walked her through it. I played the part of the perpetrator and verified that he actually reached into, or broke the plane of the doorway, reaching for and taking the money out of Helen V——'s hand. Helen V—— stated that she was positive that his hand had come inside the residence by two to three inches when he reached in to get the money. Therefore this case should be classified as a first-degree burglary.

Helen V—— got into her car and drove around the neighborhood looking for subject, however she could not locate him.

She described the subject as a H M A [Hispanic Male Adult], 40's, 5-4 thin approximately 145, with collar-length wavy black hair. He was wearing a black nylon jacket that had a square white logo over the left breast pocket, dirty Levi's that were torn at the back left leg area and dirty white tennis shoes.

The police arrested a suspect. The man arrested was another less-than-desirable resident of the airport district. He had a criminal record. Apparently, he had a prior conviction for theft at Scott Peterson's country club. I spent more than a decade of my life as a prosecutor in Los Angeles. I have worked on a lot of criminal cases. I find it very strange that there was so much suspicious criminal activity in Laci's neighborhood near the time she disappeared. This was an unusual occurrence for any neighborhood, especially this quintessentially quiet, middle-class neighborhood.

THE MEDINA BURGLARY

The most troubling and unexplainable example of the criminal activity on the day of Laci's vanishing was the burglary that took place across the street from the Peterson home on the morning of December 24, the morning Laci was last seen. The home was that of Rudy and Susan Medina.

An eyewitness saw the burglary in progress at the time and reported it promptly to the police. The burglars were later apprehended, confessed to the crime, but insisted that it had been committed during the night of December 27. They were obviously lying about the timing of the occurrence but nevertheless were permitted to plead guilty to charges framed to provide the date of the burglary as well after December 24.

Why was this allowed?

Nothing could be more certain than the fact that this crime did not occur on December 27. The plea, however, permitted them to avoid admitting they were engaged in criminal activity across the street from the Peterson home during the time period of Laci's last sighting.

The police records establish without any doubt that the burglary could not have occurred on December 27. In addition to the eyewitness who saw it take place on December 24, the victims discovered their loss on December 26 and reported it to the police on the same day.

On December 26, Officer Fainter wrote the following report:

We were called to the 523 Covena address [the Peterson home] to assist with crowd control. While we were on scene, the neighbor from 516 Covena arrived home.

The homeowners went into their home. After they were inside the house for approximately one minute, the female ran out and said that their house had been broken into. Officer Meyer and myself conducted a security check of the inside of the home. It was determined that there had been a burglary while the homeowners were gone on vacation for the Christmas holiday. Officer Wend responded to conduct the investigation of the burglary.

Officer Wend prepared a supplemental police report in which he stated, "Due to the priority to 523 Covena (Petersons) I did not contact neighbors in regards to this incident." This was consistent with the police focus on Scott Peterson and a disregard for the burglars who had been across the street as possible suspects in Laci's disappearance.

A police phone log established that a witness had seen the burglary in progress on the morning of December 24.

A police report generated early in the case by Detective Stough states:

> *On December 27th, 2002, at 1830 hours, I received information from Detective Blom and police clerk Gallagher, of information on this burglary. I was provided with a copy of the police report along with a separate typed page that indicated that at 1610 hours on 12-27-02, a Diane Jackson (via Sergeant Ed Steele) said she witnessed the 459 [the California burglary statute] on Covena on 12-24-02 at 1140 hours. She saw the van and the safe being removed from the house.*"

In other words, witness Diana Jackson stated to Sergeant Ed Steele that she saw the Medina house, which was located across the street from the Peterson home, being burglarized on December 24 at 11:40 A.M. Specifically, according to the police report, she informed Sergeant Steele that "she saw the van and the safe being removed from the house."

After an interview of Diane Jackson on December 27, 2002, about her sighting, Detective Stough of the Modesto Police Department reports as follows:

I called that number at 1830 hours and spoke with Diane Jackson. She told me that on 1140 hours on Tuesday, 12-24-02, she was driving down Covena towards her house. As she drove by the residence at 516 Covena she saw three short of stature, dark skinned but not African American guys in the front yard of the residence. She stated as she drove by the guys turned and looked at her and that they were standing near a van. When asked to further describe the individuals she stated that that's all she could remember as she wasn't thinking about that and hadn't thought about that until she called the police. I asked her if she believed that she would be able to identify any of these subjects if she saw them again and she stated she didn't know but she doubted it. I then asked her if she saw them at the back of the van or in the yard. She told me that the van was parked on the street in front of the house and not in the driveway. She stated that two of the individuals were standing at the back of the van and one was standing in the front yard near the van. She thought it unusual that they looked because she initially thought that they were

*landscapers and that landscapers normally continue
working. They don't stop and look at traffic going by.
She stated that she first told the officers she believed the
van was white but upon thinking of it more she thought
darker. I asked the witness to attempt to remember back
as she was driving by and see if she could visualize the
van in her mind. At this point she said she thought
darker, either a tan or a brown-colored van. She stated
that it was an older van and that it had a door or both
doors that opened to the rear but she didn't remember
anything else about it. I provided the witness with my
name and phone number and advised her to call and
leave any further information regardless of how in-
significant she thought it was on my voicemail and I
would respond if need be.*

Diane Jackson further stated on January 16, 2003, that she was
sure of her time, because as she drove home from the hand
therapist, she knew that her husband would be home at noon
for lunch. She said that when she pulled into her driveway, she
looked at her watch, and it was 11:40 A.M. She said that she
made a mental note to herself that she would have time to fix
her husband lunch. Mrs. Jackson stated that when she heard on
the Friday after Christmas that the Medinas' home at 516
Covena had been burglarized, she telephoned the police to tell
them what she had seen on December 24.

As noted previously, on the night of December 23, Simon
L——, a neighbor of the Petersons, was sitting in his car when

he spotted a suspicious-looking brown van. He followed the van down Encina Street in the direction of the Peterson house and sped away when a man got out of the van and started toward his car. Simon L—— said there were two other people near the back doors of the van. He called the police twice and grew frustrated and angry when no one came to take his statement. Even though this brown van matches the description of the brown van at the Woodward Reservoir and at the Medina house, apparently there was no investigation done to conclusively determine that.

Steven Todd and Donald Glenn Pearce, two men who lived in Modesto's airport district, were arrested for the Medina burglary on January 2, 2003. During a police interview, the first words out of suspect Todd's mouth were that he didn't have anything to do with "the woman."

The beginning of the police report indicates, "Todd immediately stated that he would tell me about the burglary but he had nothing to do with the woman. When I asked Todd what woman he was talking about, he stated that it was the missing woman with the baby. I again asked Todd to tell me about the burglary."

By making this unsolicited statement, it appears that Todd assumed he was being questioned regarding Laci. It appears from this officer's lack of follow-up into Todd's statement regarding "the missing woman with the baby" that the police viewed these incidents as separate and unrelated.

Remember, a police report states that when Susan Medina

returned to her home on December 26, she realized the home had been broken into and yelled, "I've been robbed."

An officer at the Peterson house came over, and she told him what happened.

Yet Steven Todd said to police that he started stealing property from the Medinas' backyard on December 27 at 3:00 A.M. Eventually, he said he kicked in the French doors in the back. He says he took the safe that night.

From the police report:

Todd stated that at approximately 0300 hours, in the early morning of 12-27-02, he rode his bicycle back to the residence at 516 Covena. Todd stated that when he arrived on Covena, he parked his bicycle near a fence located on the south side of the residence. Todd said he propped his bicycle up against the fence and jumped over into the back yard. Todd said that while he was in the back yard, he immediately started looking around a shed located near the back of the house. The shed door was open, and Todd went inside and selected several items that included air tools, Craftsman hand tools, an air stapler, an air compressor, a weed eater, and an air blower.

Todd carried off the air tools, hand tools, and weed eater. Then, he says he got back on his bicycle and rode back to the home, where he removed a safe from the house. He woke Pearce and told him that he needed help retrieving the safe. Pearce got up, and the two returned to the Medinas' house in Pearce's white sedan.

Witness Diane Jackson told the police she saw a safe being placed in "either a tan or a brown-colored van" the morning of December 24, at approximately the same time Scott said Laci would have been out walking. They did not believe the burglary to be related to Laci's disappearance.

A CALL FROM PRISON

The suspicion surrounding these Medina burglars continued to develop.

Two weeks after Laci's disappearance, a prison corrections officer heard a taped telephone conversation between an inmate and his brother regarding Laci Peterson. Modesto PD received a copy of the taped phone call, but somehow that tape disappeared.

This is from an investigator's report after he spoke with Xavier Aponte, a lieutenant with the California Department of Corrections.

> *Lt. Aponte first became aware of [inmate] Ted J——*
> *talking about Laci Peterson within a couple of weeks of*
> *her missing. [Ted J——] was talking about Laci missing*
> *while he was out in his housing unit. A housing staff per-*
> *son left a message on Lt. Aponte's voice mail, and he*
> *immediately called the Modesto Police Department hot-*
> *line. He called a second time within the same week be-*

cause he did not receive a call back from his first tele-
phone call. Lt. Aponte said it was at least a week before
anyone got back to him. Lt. Aponte said a detective
called him back, and arrangements were made for the
detective to interview Ted J——. Lt. Aponte believes
that it was after he spoke to the detective that he listened
to the recorded conversation between Ted J—— and his
brother (name not given). To the best of his recollection,
Ted J—— talked to [brother] about Laci Peterson miss-
ing and [brother] mentioned that Laci happened to
walk up while Steve Todd was doing the burglary and
Todd made some type of verbal threat to Laci.

Modesto police came to the California Rehabilitation Center
and interviewed the inmate within the first couple of weeks following Lieutenant Aponte's call to the hotline. Aponte said that
the inmate appeared scared. He denied having a conversation
with his brother and denied knowing Steve Todd.

Immediately following his interview with the Modesto detective, the inmate went back to his unit and phoned his
mother's home, trying to get in touch with his brother. According to Aponte, he told his mother to tell his brother that the police had just interviewed him and he was to keep his mouth shut
because, "You don't know who you're dealing with."

Is it possible that Laci interrupted the burglary at the Medina home? The inmate was not talking and nothing further was
developed regarding these mysterious circumstances.

What can account for law enforcement's failure to demand

an explanation from the admitted burglars as to why they claimed the burglary occurred on a date which had to have been false and had to have been known so by law enforcement. The victims of the burglary, the eyewitness, and the Modesto Police Department were on record that the date of the burglary could not be December 27. There was information that one of the burglars had threatened Laci.

Not only was this issue not pursued but the charges against the burglars were framed in such a way to permit them to stick to this false claim by charging that the offense occurred sometime over a three-day period.

The disposition of the criminal case against them was equally curious. In the eyes of the law some of the most dangerous criminals are those who enter occupied residences in the nighttime to commit crimes. Although still serious, it is a lesser offense to burglarize an unoccupied residence in the daytime. By falsely claiming that they broke in by kicking in the French doors at night while the Medinas were home, they would have ordinarily aggravated their already gravely serious position.

Todd pleaded guilty to one burglary count and Donald Pearce, his codefendant, pleaded guilty to a reduced charge of receiving stolen property. Todd was a "third striker," having suffered three prior convictions for residential burglary. He should have been prosecuted under the California three-strikes law. The prosecution had a very strong case against him, considering that he confessed to committing the burglary at the Medina house. He should have received a sentence of twenty-five years to life.

Instead, the same prosecutor who was prosecuting Scott Peterson gave him a bargain of eight years and eight months. Pearce, the other participant convicted in the Medina burglary, received only 180 days in the county jail, his charge reduced from the serious three-strikes law offense of first-degree residential burglary to a lesser charge of receiving stolen property.

Here then is the plea bargain. You say you broke into an occupied house in the nighttime instead of an unoccupied house in the daytime, and you avoid a third strike and the codefendant avoids prison entirely.

Such a plea bargain is marvelous for the criminals but a very poor result for crime victims and potential crime victims.

What motivated such generosity on the part of the prosecution?

How could they believe the burglars' story that they committed the crime on the twenty-seventh?

Todd had even offered to testify that he saw "Mr. Peterson" get into his truck and drive away from his home in the early-morning hours. This would fit in nicely with the police theory of Laci's body being removed from the home at the same time that Todd would have apparently been casing the neighborhood for possible burglary opportunities.

I would guess that the prosecutors decided no jury would believe his story of sighting Scott Peterson under such circumstances, and decided that this would be carrying the matter a bit too far.

In working out this resolution of the case, a preliminary hearing was avoided. No testimony was taken—no public hearing that would show the falsity of the burglars' claim as to when the crime was committed.

However this result occurred, it permitted two otherwise impermissible interpretations of the facts: First, the Medina burglary occurred well after December 24 and thus was unrelated to Laci's disappearance, leaving the focus on Scott; second, the burglars were relieved of admitting their presence at the scene at the time of her disappearance.

Were there others besides Medina burglars Steve Todd and Donald Pearce involved in the burglary? A brown van, a white van, and a white Chevrolet sedan, which the burglars said they had used, were seen by witnesses on December 24 at the Medina house when the Medinas were on vacation. Only two people, Todd and Pearce, were convicted in the burglary. Perhaps a check for fingerprints of the hammer, the dolly, or the safe would have helped identify others involved in the burglary.

ANOTHER PREGNANT WOMAN IS TERRORIZED

At noon on December 24, a woman who was eight months pregnant was opening her store on Yosemite Boulevard, five blocks from the Peterson house. Two men in a red Toyota Corolla, both with tattoos, and one wearing a beanie cap, terrorized her. She reported that they watched her as she was opening her shop. They continued to sit in their car and observe her for about forty-five minutes as she set up the displays in front of the store. Then they started their car up, drove around the block, and parked across the street. She said she was the only one visible inside her shop.

At that point, the driver pulled his car in front of the store, and both men got out of their car and started toward her business. She immediately ran toward the back of the store and asked a male employee to come out with her. He did, and then he called the police.

All that appears in the discovery is a short dispatch log reference showing the phone call that came in to the police department on December 24. The log indicates the license plate number of the suspicious vehicle and to whom it was registered. There was no apparent follow-up.

The suspicious car was registered to someone who lived in the airport district, just a block away from the two men involved in the burglary at the Medina home. This made me wonder whether the airport district criminals engaging in simultaneous felonious conduct in Laci's neighborhood at the time of her disappearance knew one another. I reported what I'd learned to Mark Geragos.

POSSIBLE LEADS

Picture the Peterson neighborhood around the time of Laci's disappearance. Six possible felonies were all occurring there between the evening of December 23 and afternoon of December 24. We have questionable people from the airport district going door to door posing as neighbors and asking for money.

We have the burglary at the Medina home, a burglary resulting in generous plea bargains for Steven Todd and Donald Glen Pearce, both of the airport district as well.

A brown van was described in a possible attempted abduction the night of the twenty-third, a daytime burglary the morning of the twenty-fourth, and possibly the satanic rape and abduction days before Laci disappeared. The group in the van at the Woodward Reservoir was from the airport district of Modesto.

On the afternoon of December 24, a woman eight months pregnant was terrorized by two men in a car, five blocks from where Laci was last seen alive. She told me that she thought they were trying to "get" her. She got the license plate number of the vehicle, and it was registered to a residence in the airport district—a few blocks from where the other criminals lived.

That day was not calm. It was not peaceful and certainly not your typical day before Christmas in Modesto, California. However, none of what I discovered was apparently pursued as the case continued to build against Scott Peterson.

The conviction of Scott Peterson occupied center stage.

My frustration grew with every new piece of evidence I uncovered.

4

CREDIBLE WITNESSES

Six eyewitnesses I interviewed were convinced that they saw Laci Peterson alive and well after she was supposed to have disappeared. None of these witnesses testified at trial.

Geragos cross-examined the police about their knowledge of these witnesses and what they reported, but the court correctly instructed the jury that they could not consider this for the truth of what the witnesses said because it constituted hearsay. That meant that in their deliberations the jury was precluded from considering that six witnesses claimed to have seen Laci walking her dog on the morning of December 24. If even one witness had convinced the jury of this fact, Scott should have been exonerated, since it would have established that Laci was alive well after Scott had left home.

Police testified that these sightings of Laci were not a priority for the investigation. They had, however, issued a press release asking for witnesses who may have seen Scott the day Laci disappeared, and they used the media to publicize pictures of his boat and truck. Clearly, it was not a priority to investigate any evidence that did not support their theory of the crime.

Geragos said in his opening statement that the witnesses would be called. I do not know why they were not. These are decisions that can be made only by the trial lawyer. In his final argument, the prosecutor argued that the failure to produce the witnesses was not the responsibility of the prosecution but rather that of the defense.

THE FIRST SIGHTING

Homer and Helen Maldonado said that they spotted Laci between approximately 9:50 A.M. and 10:00 A.M. on December 24, 2002. Homer Maldonado told me that he and his wife drove to the USA Mini Mart gas station on Miller Avenue, near the corner of Covena and Miller. Maldonado said that after they left the gas station, they drove west on Miller past Covena. At that time, they observed a beautiful young woman whom he described as being "very pregnant." She was walking a golden retriever and appeared to be having trouble controlling him; the dog pranced on his back legs, and his front paws were up as if he were jumping up on her.

Maldonado remembers asking his wife if she saw the pregnant woman having trouble with her dog.

"I hope she doesn't fall," Helen said.

After seeing photographs of Laci Peterson, Maldonado was convinced that she was the woman. Although he did not know the family, he contacted both the police and Laci's brother, Brent Rocha, saying that he had seen Laci alive on the twenty-fourth.

Maldonado saw the woman he later identified as Laci Peterson at about the second house from the corner from Miller Avenue, on the west side of the street. He produced receipts proving that he was in the area at the time that he said he was.

Maldonado telephoned the Modesto police on January 1, 2003, but claims he did not receive a call back. He then went to the command post to report the sighting. He said he was told that a detective would talk to him. According to Maldonado, no one did. He also claims to have repeated the story to the police chaplain.

THE BREAD TRUCK DRIVER

On January 20, an investigator working with us was contacted by Tony Freitas, a route driver for Orowheat bread. Freitas told him that on December 24, 2002, he was driving down La Loma Avenue on his usual route to deliver to Denny's restaurant.

Freitas said that he saw a pregnant woman walking a golden retriever. He'd noticed her on his route before. Later, after seeing Laci's photo in the paper, he recognized her as the woman with the dog. Freitas estimated the time was between 9:00 A.M. and 10:00 A.M. The woman was walking on the south side of the street, heading west, toward town. She was across the street from a triangular-shaped parklike area close to the Miller Avenue intersection. This was just around the corner from where Maldonado made his sighting.

Freitas recalled seeing two "scraggily" looking males at the bus stop bench beside the grassy area.

He called police as soon as he realized that the woman he saw on December 24 was Laci Peterson. No one from the police department returned his call, he said.

RECOGNIZING LACI

Neighbor Martha Aguilar had no problem recognizing Laci. She estimated she spotted her walking the dog between 9:45 A.M. and 10:00 A.M. on December 24 while she drove on La Loma.

Aguilar, who lived a few blocks from the Petersons, told us that she knew Laci because they went to the same doctor. I verified her statement that she and Laci did indeed go to the same doctor. According to Aguilar, the Modesto police never followed up on her call.

TWO CALLS TO THE POLICE

The Modesto police dispatch log shows two calls from Gene Pedrioli, who spotted a woman whom he thought was Laci about the same time as the other witnesses did. He had to pick up a prescription at his pharmacy at 10:00 A.M. and noticed the golden retriever because it was the same color as his own dog.

The pregnant woman with the dog was in the same area as where Aguilar had spotted her. Tree branches blocked the path on the sidewalk, and she and the dog walked around them.

When he talked to the police, Pedrioli was told to get proof that he was where he said he was. Basically, he told me, he felt he was being ignored. He gave up trying to convince police.

THE COUNCILMAN'S WIFE

I spent more time with Vivian Mitchell than I did with any of the other witnesses. A charming woman in her late seventies, she was positive that the woman and dog she'd seen were Laci and McKenzie. She recognized them from pictures in the newspapers and had seen them walking in the neighborhood several times before.

As she stood at her kitchen window the morning of December 24, Mitchell watched them for approximately four minutes, she told me.

She remembered that her husband had been watching a football game and that it was approximately 10:30 A.M.

"Bill, there's that lady with the pretty dog," Mitchell told her husband, a former Modesto city council member.

The window faced La Sombra Avenue, and Mitchell said that the woman was walking her dog east, approaching Buena Vista Drive. When they reached the corner, the dog tried to go south on Buena Vista, and Laci was trying to go in the opposite direction.

Once Laci got the dog turned around, they walked north on Buena Vista toward La Loma Avenue.

When she telephoned the police approximately a week later and told them what she saw, the woman she spoke with at the police department did not seem very interested, Mitchell told me. *I* was interested, however.

Because of her age, we were going to do a conditional examination, which means taking her testimony under oath in order to preserve it. If the worst happened, and she was unavailable to come to court, her statement could have been admitted as evidence at the trial and considered by the jury. This was never accomplished.

Sadly, Vivian Mitchell died before the trial. Her statement was never preserved, and a valuable witness was lost.

HOSPITAL EMPLOYEE

Diana Campos, a custodian at Stanislaus County Hospital, was taking a break from work and standing overlooking Moose Park, approximately fifty yards from where she saw a pregnant woman walking her dog on the morning of December 24.

The woman was walking west, away from two men who were five to ten feet behind her. Campos watched them for approximately five minutes. The dog was constantly barking. One of the men, who was wearing a beanie, shouted, "Shut the fucking dog up!"

Campos thought it odd that a man would swear at a pregnant woman. Later, she saw a flyer of Laci Peterson and realized that it was the same woman she had seen with the men. She contacted the hospital security department, and the police took her statement.

Campos said she is "good with faces" and that she is certain that it was Laci. She used to watch her friend's golden retriever, Campos said, and is certain it was a golden retriever the woman was walking. She also identified a white spot on the dog's chest similar to the one on the Petersons' dog, McKenzie.

I decided to walk the path through the park near the Kerwin Bridge, the same area where Laci was last seen. It gets really thick with bushes as you head on the path back toward Laci's house. The Peterson house is about ten short blocks from this location. I continued to make my way down the path when a man came out of the bushes next to the path. I was right where

Laci would have been when Campos spotted her, and I did what she may have tried to do: I took off walking in the opposite direction.

A public bathroom is located near the area where Campos said she saw Laci. A Modesto police report indicated that an unidentified witness heard screaming coming from that bathroom the morning of December 24. Police dismissed the information and reported it was "a rumor." Once again, anything that didn't pertain to Scott's guilt was often not pursued.

It's unusual to have this many witnesses come forward in a case, but certainly this case was far from ordinary. If it hadn't been for the publicity the case received, it never would have happened. As it was, many people reported what they saw, and the witnesses all came forward with their observations soon after learning of Laci's disappearance. In my opinion, they were credible witnesses, and they were all convinced that they'd seen Laci Peterson on December 24.

Yet apparently the police spoke to only one of these witnesses. More than seventy officers were taking calls. From what I could see in the discovery, the only calls referred to Brocchini and Grogan were those pertaining to Scott Peterson.

It did not appear to me that these six witnesses who reported they saw Laci walking her dog the morning of the twenty-fourth were mistaken. There were no other reports of a pregnant women walking a golden retriever at that time in the area where Laci was seen. Besides, this was Laci's normal walking route—almost a perfect circle around the neighborhood equaling a distance of just about a mile. These witnesses did not know that.

These witnesses convinced me. They were respectable, intelligent citizens with no motive to misrepresent what they saw.

5

THE AUTOPSY REPORT

I could no longer afford to stay at a hotel. Since I was living in Modesto, it was difficult getting my paychecks, and my out-of-pocket expenses were starting to add up. Because the hotel was too expensive, Mark Geragos rented office space in downtown Modesto above the J Street Café. The building, conveniently located one block from the jail, had to date from the early 1900s. There was a communal bathroom down the hall with a toilet and a sink. We didn't have a phone, fax, or copier. I had to go across the street to make copies or send faxes. I relied on my brothers, Jack, a teacher, and Bart, a lawyer, to do my Internet research. Our inadequate resources were a serious handicap. I had never experienced this as a government lawyer.

As I slept on the carpeted floor the first night I spent in my new "home," I felt something scurry across my chest in the middle of the night. Mouse, I thought. Or worse, rat. From that point on, I actually slept in a tent.

Although I had never been to Modesto before, I soon began to realize that there was a darker side to the tranquil San Joaquin Valley city. All I really knew about the city was that earlier Mark Geragos had handled another high-profile case there. In 2001, popular congressman Gary Condit—whose supporters used the term *Condit Country* to describe the area—made headlines when his affair with missing congressional intern Chandra Levy was revealed.

Condit had hired Geragos to defend his reputation to the media. His political career was ruined by the scandal anyway, although police said he was not a suspect in Levy's disappearance and murder, which remains unsolved. Now Geragos was representing Scott Peterson, and I would get an opportunity to explore a side of the city that most people didn't see.

With a population of more than two hundred thousand, Modesto is the fifteenth largest city in California. The seat of Stanislaus County, the largely agricultural community is located ninety miles east of San Francisco. Farther to the east lie the foothills of Gold Country, the Sierra Nevada Mountain Range, and Yosemite National Park.

Like many towns in the Central Valley, Modesto is a city of farmers' markets, orchards, and fruit stands. Birthplace of filmmaker George Lucas, it tries to live up to its *American Graffiti* image every June with '60s-themed concerts, classic-car parades, and street fairs during Graffiti Summer.

Upon entering the city of Modesto, one is met by a huge sign that says: WATER WEALTH CONTENTMENT HEALTH. The contentment level was running pretty low during the months I spent there. The Modesto I saw was fueled by grief and, most of all, anger. Citizens by the thousands mourned Laci and donated blood in her memory, and most of them instinctively hated anyone with any connection to Scott Peterson.

As the Peterson story dominated the news, I realized that I had taken on one of the least popular jobs in the country. In a short time, I had already received hate e-mails—all unsigned, of course—with messages like:

Hey, Matt . . . if your boy is really innocent, why don't you have him take a lie detector test? Meanwhile, the smoke and mirrors sideshow you and your cohorts are staging is hilarious!

All of the hostility directed at me changed my perspective as to what I was doing in Modesto. I realized that a lot of people were following this case with great passion. There was a strong public perception that Scott had murdered Laci, and I think a lot of it was because of the relentless media coverage and its prejudicial nature.

These people don't know what I know, I thought. Certainly

many would share my concerns once they realized that there were numerous unanswered questions and suspicious circumstances suggesting the involvement of others and a lack of convincing evidence of Scott Peterson's guilt. I truly felt that I was working just as much for Laci by bringing to justice whoever had abducted her.

However, it continued to be apparent that the police and the public's presumption of guilt was so strong that the burden was shifting from the prosecution to establish guilt to the defense to establish innocence—that is, to show that someone else had committed this crime and who this was.

As the lead-up to the trial continued, emotions became even more intense. Two radio talk-show personalities pondered on-air, "What kind of mothers could have given birth to Mark Geragos and Matt Dalton?" and described us as "the devil's spawn."

My tires were slashed when I was visiting Peterson, with my car parked right outside the jail. The manager of the Red Lion asked Jackie and Lee Peterson to move out. He was later fired.

One night while I was dining alone in a Modesto restaurant, a man walked up to my table and asked, "Are you Scott Peterson's lawyer?" Before I could respond, he went on to say, "I think Scott Peterson is guilty as hell, and he should die for what he did." Having said his piece, he stormed out.

Another time I was walking to the jail to see Scott when two men in a truck pulled up beside me. They apparently recognized me as someone connected to Scott Peterson, because they slowed way down and began yelling profanities at me. It went on for a little while. The last thing I heard was one of them yelling, "He did it!"

I told Scott about these confrontations. I knew that there had been similar hostility, some of it life threatening, directed at him after Laci's disappearance. Police reports in the case confirm this. The hostility toward him came not just from those living in Modesto; it was from all over the country.

For example, there is this police report from Detective Grogan:

> *On Wednesday, 2-12-2003 at 1000 hours, I received a telephone call from Sharon ROCHA. Sharon told me she had received four messages on her telephone from Terry P—— who told her "just give me the word and I'll take care of Scott." Sharon was concerned that the individual was offering to kill Scott PETERSON and thought she should inform me of this.*

I remembered what I had been told about someone driving a truck through Peterson's office door. If he had been in his office that day, he could have been killed. Early in their investigation, police released pictures of his truck and boat to the public, asking if anyone had seen him on or about December 24. False leaks to the media about the smell of bleach in the house and evidence of four missing anchors fueled the passionate feelings people already had regarding the case.

These and other confrontations made me realize how

emotionally involved many people were with this case. Maybe it was "O.J. backlash," as the media has suggested. Or maybe, lacking other suspects, the public, as well as the police, wanted to believe that Peterson's extramarital affair and his absence of visible, public mourning meant that he was capable of murder.

THE BODIES SPEAK

Laci Peterson's autopsy was completed on May 14, 2003. We received the coroner's report on June 12, 2003, following a procedural court appearance in Modesto. Mark usually brought a group of other lawyers up to Modesto with him from Los Angeles when we had court appearances. This time was no exception. Afterward we caravanned two carloads of people to the outskirts of town and ate lunch. Mark skimmed through the autopsy report and then passed it off to a lawyer friend of his who was assisting us for the day.

Frustrated, Bill Pavelic and I watched them reading without commenting until Pavelic announced that he and I had an interview scheduled with a potential witness.

We stood up and started to leave when Pavelic reached out for the report and said, "Matt and I will make copies."

He'd read my mind.

We then jumped into my car and left.

As I drove, he began reading the report aloud.

AUTOPSY FINDINGS

Female body with:

A. Absence of each radius, each ulna, and both hands

B. Absence of both feet and left tibia and fibula

C. Absence of head and cervical vertebrae 1–6

D. Absence of thoracoabdominal viscera

2. Gravid uterus; fetus, placenta, and umbilical cord absent, with opening near fundus. Cervix intact and closed.

3. Extensive changes of immersion, postmortem animal feeding, tidal effect, and decomposition; estimated postmortem interval: months.

4. Multiple rib fractures (left 5 and 6, right 9)

CAUSE OF DEATH: Undetermined

This was the first I had heard that Laci's hands, feet, and head were missing.

I also learned that she had duct tape on her thighs. Laci may have been restrained with duct tape. This was a key piece of physical evidence. Duct tape is a commonly used tool in abduction cases. It's quick, it's cheap, it's easier than trying to tie rope, and, if done right, it's almost impossible for the victim to escape.

When I was working for the district attorney's office, I prosecuted a handful of abduction cases. One involved a truck driver who, when hauling a load of stereo equipment, was abducted by men in a van. They duct taped his hands and feet together, took his truck, and drove him five miles to North Long

Beach, where they stuffed him into a shed. He was found twelve hours later.

Another case I prosecuted involved juvenile gang members in East Los Angeles who kidnapped a security guard after engaging in an armed robbery. They duct taped his hands, feet, and mouth, and drove him to the harbor area, where they dropped him off. He survived. A passerby found him in the middle of a field.

There were many cases like these in the Los Angeles District Attorney's Office. The presence of duct tape suggests the possibility of an abduction. The police, however, sought only to link Scott to the duct tape by comparing it to the tape on flyers he had posted regarding the then missing Laci. What would it have shown if it had been compared with the duct tape found in the brown van? What could account for the multiple rib fractures if this had been a "soft kill," as was the police's prevailing theory?

According to the autopsy report, the condition of the baby was remarkably different from Laci's remains:

> The body is that of a decomposed male fetus. . . . As received, 1½ loops of plastic tape are around the neck of the fetus, with extension to a knot near the left shoulder.
>
> The skin is uninjured beneath this loop and slack between the loops, and the neck is roughly 2 cm. Examination of the chest reveals an apparent postmortem tear exposing the internal surfaces of the right shoulder and the right hemithorax. This injury extends onto the right lateral ab-

dominal wall with partial evisceration of small and large intestine. . . .

AUTOPSY DIAGNOSES

1. Phenotypic male fetus, estimated gestational age 9 months (33–38 weeks based on anthropologic measurements)
2. No gross external or internal anomalies
3. Moderate postmortem decomposition with apparent additional postmortem injuries to torso; no evidence of animal feeding

CAUSE OF DEATH: Undetermined

COMMENT: Moderate decomposition without evidence of postmortem animal feeding suggests relative protection of this body prior to its discovery.

The condition of the baby raised some unusual questions with no satisfactory explanations.

The one and a half loops of plastic tape around the neck contained a knot. The fact that there was only two centimeters of slack between the tape and the baby's neck meant that the tape, in my opinion, could not possibly have floated over the head. How, then, did it get there?

In the autopsy photos there also appeared to be a piece of electrical tape, squared off at the end, holding the baby's ear folded over. The police claimed that the material was seaweed. I have lived on or near California beaches all my life and have never seen seaweed that looked like that. I have never seen sea-weed that can stick and hold down a human ear. The "seaweed" was never produced for us to examine.

When I viewed the body months after he had been found, what appeared to me to be an adhesive mark was still on his face. You could see what looked like the perforations consistent with tape being cut off. Unfortunately, this was never expertly tested.

It seemed clear to me in that photo that the Peterson baby's ear was held down with black electrical tape. This, in addition to the clear plastic twine wrapped around the baby's neck and chest, indicated the baby had been handled by someone. This did not fit the prosecution theory of the "soft kill."

Geragos and I met Rick Distaso and Stanislaus County Senior Deputy District Attorney Dave Harris at Modesto PD with the intention of taking close-up photos of the forensic evidence and having a knot expert look at the knot around the baby's neck and chest to see if it was man-made. We believed that the expert might help us in figuring out where that object around the baby's neck came from and how it was wrapped so closely around the baby. We were shocked to see that it had become untied, destroying what I think was significant evidence.

The material holding down the baby's ear was a key piece of evidence, in my opinion. If it was in fact black electrical tape, it could have been tested for fingerprint evidence. Fingerprint evidence is almost impossible to refute, and had there been any on the tape, it could have told us a great deal. I met at once with the Contra Costa coroner. When the bodies arrived at her office, there was no tape on the baby, the coroner told me. She knew nothing about the tape, and there had been no mention of it to her.

I then showed the coroner the picture of the baby with what appeared to be tape on his ear and material wrapped around his neck and chest. She said she had never seen either of the items that were attached to the baby. Whatever was holding down the ear disappeared after Richmond police took the picture. Who got rid of it? And why?

At the time the bodies were discovered, a pallet bag—a huge, plastic bag designed to cover a six-foot pallet—was found washed up in the same area. The bag also had duct tape attached to it. A few feet away were metal pipes with duct tape attached.

Even more compelling was the observation made by East Bay Regional Park District police officer Timothy Phillips that the pallet bag's odor was similar to that of the remains. This important information was not contained in any police reports that I reviewed.

If the baby's body had been placed in the pallet bag, it would explain the lesser extent of decomposition as well as the odor noticed by Officer Phillips.

I found a report in the discovery documenting the police investigation into the bag. In the report, Detective Brocchini wrote that he called the Canadian company that manufactured the pallet cover bags, Target Products, and asked them if they shipped their product to Modesto. The company did not. Brocchini's investigation of the bag apparently ended there. It didn't fit into the prosecution's theory about Scott Peterson, so apparently it was not pursued.

I conducted my own investigation into the bag and its origins. I called Target Products and asked where they shipped pallets of their product; I was told they shipped to the San Francisco Bay. In fact, their product was being used on the Richmond Bridge retrofitting project near where the bodies were found.

"The bag did not blow off a ship," the representative told me. "We transport those bags from Canada all the way to San Francisco. I don't know how it could make it all that way and then suddenly blow off when it reached its destination. Also, we don't put duct tape on the pallet cover bags—none of them. Someone else did that, not us."

I drove to the Richmond Bridge construction site. The construction site was secured with barbed-wire fencing, and at night the grounds were patrolled by security guards. I had a contact who was working on the project, and he was able to get me access to the site.

I saw the Target pallet cover bags on the premises. I wanted to find out how someone could possibly come into possession of one of these bags. I asked a foreman what was done with the Target pallet cover bags after they were finished with them, and he said they were thrown into a Dumpster and eventually taken to the Richmond Sanitation Company, located a short distance from where the bodies and bag had washed up.

I went to the Richmond Sanitation Company. It would be easy for someone off the street to come in there, I thought. I noticed that there were security cameras pointed at the landfill. I asked the manager if I could look at his security tapes starting from the week of December 24, 2002. He told me to get a subpoena.

We eventually served Richmond Sanitation with a subpoena demanding their videotapes for the period Laci went missing. They later claimed that they had taped over the days we requested. The tapes were lost forever.

The next morning, I went to the jail as early as I could get in, around 7:00 or 7:30. I wanted to tell Scott about the autopsy report and about all the physical evidence we hadn't known about before.

"This is pretty graphic," I told him, indicating the report, "but I think we may be on to something critical."

Just then my phone rang. It was Mark checking in. There was no way I wanted to excitedly repeat it all right there in front of Scott. The details were gruesome, even if they were very helpful to our case.

"Close your ears," I told him and watched as he walked to the other side of the room and put his fingers in his ears. I would tell him the gist of my findings later, sparing him the unnecessary details about his wife's and child's remains. To Mark, I said, "Laci disappears on December twenty-fourth. She doesn't have hands or feet. Her head is missing. The baby has a slash on the chest, but something kept the animal life from feeding on him. The baby may have been inside the pallet cover bag and weighted down by the metal pipes, and we have to have the bag tested."

I also let Mark know that Laci tested positive for caffeine. Laci didn't drink caffeine because of her pregnancy. How had it gotten into her system? Had she been kept alive?

I finished the call and then told Scott in a less vivid way what I had told Mark. His reaction was what you would expect from a grief-stricken husband. The information in the autopsy report kept Scott awake at night. He stopped eating, and his physical appearance reflected the emotional damage the report had done to him.

The evidence from the autopsy report, had it been revealed earlier, might have caused the police to try to find if anyone had handled the baby. But now it appeared to be too late. The police had long been convinced that Scott Peterson was their man.

They were continuing to drag the bay at this time, looking for cement anchors to establish that their weight had dismembered Laci's body. Not one anchor was ever found.

In the meantime, I believed that I had found evidence indicating that others might have been responsible for the deaths of Laci and Conner.

6

CULTS AND COINCIDENCES

Because of the hostility I was facing in Modesto, and because we couldn't afford to hire anyone, I decided to call Brad, a longtime friend, to accompany me on some of the interviews I was doing out in the airport district. Now that Brad was there, I felt a lot more comfortable in Modesto.

When he came to town, the temperature was 109 degrees. I had been sleeping on the floor of the office, protected by my tent from scurrying rodents. I had soon learned that I was staying next door to what became a nightclub on Friday and Saturday nights. Brad arrived on a Friday, and we decided to go down to the nightclub and talk to some of the local people and find out what we could about the town.

We met a group of young girls who had grown up in Modesto. I asked one of them, a college student at California State University, Stanislaus, whether there was a lot of satanic cult activity in Modesto.

"A lot of the kids around here are into occult games like this," she said, as she pointed to several groups sitting on the ground behind the nightclub, playing a game that resembled Dungeons and Dragons. "Some of these people really believe this stuff. The more hardcore element hangs out in the airport district. Those people are way out there. I stay away from them."

A berobed young man with long black hair walked by. Skull-and-crossbones earrings dangled from his earlobes, and a patch of hair sprouted from his chin.

"Is that the devil?" my friend asked.

I laughed.

Many of the patrons were dressed like that. There was definitely a theme to the evening.

"Is this a satanic night, or is it always like this?" I asked.

"Same people, same thing," one of the girls in the group said.

She went on to explain that the airport district was where a lot of people went for their drugs, which was something I already knew. An agent from the federal Drug Enforcement Agency (DEA) had told me that California's Central Valley manufactured a large percentage of the methamphetamine in the United States.

The following night, according to the satanic calendar, was a ritual day of death known as the Night the Demon Revels. I thought it would be an excellent opportunity to visit the airport district and look for some unusual activity. Brad and I were driving up and down the dirty streets of the airport area when we decided to call on my new source, Billy J——, to find out if he had seen his ex-wife or former in-laws.

As we drove by, we could see a Modesto Police Department patrol car parked in the driveway to Billy's house. What looked like an undercover police car was also parked there. We went down the street, made a U-turn, came back, and parked across the street, a few hundred feet away. Detectives Brocchini and Grogan, followed by an officer in uniform, walked to the undercover car. We watched the police drive away, then we went up to the house. I asked Billy what that was all about.

He told us that the police were asking what the Peterson investigator wanted.

"They wanted to know what I told you," he said. "I told them that you were asking about my in-laws, and whether they could have been involved in an abduction.

"Look," he continued, "these people are into weird stuff. I don't know what they're doing now because I haven't been part of that family for a while. Nothing would surprise me with them."

The son was incredibly strong and extremely unpredictable, Billy said. He looked at my friend Brad, who is a fairly large man.

"He would take you down like that," he told Brad, snapping his fingers.

Billy said he wasn't certain if the cruelty-to-animals charge that led to his former brother-in-law's arrest and jail time was satanic in nature. What he did know was that the man was cruel.

Billy's mother, a woman in her seventies, came and joined us. She stated, "My former daughter-in-law and the whole bunch of them are on drugs. One day, when Peggy [the mother] was high and coming at me, I took a swing with a two-by-four. Almost hit her in the head."

Encouraged by my laughter, she added, "The back side of Woodward Reservoir, that's where you'll find that group. That's where they live. They hunt and fish for their food, and they only come to the airport district now to get their drugs."

She then proceeded to sit us down and tell us about the family. She even gave us pictures. She knew them well from her son's former marriage and the close proximity of their residences at the time. They had lived in the airport district, right around the corner from each other.

"They are all far gone on drugs; probably meth, like a lot of other people I know around here," she said.

"Do they know Todd and Pearce, the two men who were convicted of doing the burglary across from Laci's?" I asked.

Billy walked me across his front yard and showed me where the two burglars lived—almost directly behind him and his mother.

"See, that's where their group hangs out," he said.

A report by Detective George Stough of the Modesto Police Department identified that address in the airport district as the place where the suspect, Steven Todd, lived. His cohort in the Medina burglary, Donald Pearce, lived in a trailer on the property, the detective wrote.

Stough continued his report by stating that the safe taken in the Medina burglary was supposed to be at that house where Steve Todd was staying. Also associated with the house, the detective wrote, was Alan B——, who had the numbers *666* tattooed on his forehead, and two other men.

I asked if they had seen the man with the 666 tattoo on his forehead. I didn't have to explain to them that 666 was the universal sign of the devil.

Billy said that he'd seen the man I was talking about around Steve Todd's house but didn't know who he was. He thought he lived in their neighborhood, because he used to be around a lot, always on foot.

"Most of the guys around here know each other," he said. "That whole group vanished around the time the Peterson girl disappeared."

Did Todd call upon others to help him? Witnesses described three different vehicles in front of the burglarized house on December 24. It appeared others besides just Todd and Pearce were involved. Did Alan B——, the satanist with the 666 on his forehead, assist in the burglary across the street from Laci's when she went walking the morning of the twenty-fourth? Modesto police have documented his association with burglars Todd and Pearce. Was Alan B—— connected to the group from the airport district who promised a Christmas Day murder or the two men from the airport district who terrorized the pregnant woman blocks from Laci's house on the twenty-fourth?

I wished I knew the answers, but I didn't. And unlike the government, I lacked the ability to find out.

How hardcore was this man, I wondered, to blatantly have a 666 tattoo on his forehead? As a Los Angeles prosecutor, I have seen all sorts of criminals with all sorts of different tattoos. Diehard gang members like to show gang pride by putting their tattoos in conspicuous places on their bodies. It appeared that Alan B—— had strong beliefs about Satan. Where was he on the twenty-fourth when Laci disappeared? Why did Detective Stough take notice of Alan B——'s association with burglars Todd and Pearce? Why didn't Modesto police follow up on this lead? And why had everyone in this group disappeared?

Billy pointed toward Todd's house. "I'm not involved in that crazy group behind me," he said. "I just hear things."

"What else have you heard?" I asked, suspecting that he wanted to tell me more.

"I heard that a woman named Donna—who I think lives with Todd and that group—went to the Modesto Police Department with jewelry taken in the burglary," he said. "She was told to throw it into the lobby and run."

The Modesto police confirmed this incident did in fact occur after Laci disappeared. However, they apparently did not follow up. Although there were security cameras inside the department lobby, police said the tape of the person in the lobby was not preserved. This meant a positive identification of her would be difficult to make.

Several suspects were seen across the street from Laci's on

December 24. Did Todd really confront Laci, as the inmate described it to his brother while on the phone from the California Rehabilitation Center? Was one of the suspect vehicles seen across the street from Laci's house used to abduct her? And did others in the group try to distance themselves from any involvement by returning the jewelry to the police?

Remember that burglar Steve Todd started off his statement to the police with the unsolicited line, "I had nothing to do with the woman."

The officer then proceeded to question him on the burglary only. There is no indication that he was pressed as to why he claimed the burglary occurred on the twenty-seventh, when it was clear that was false.

I asked Billy to talk to Donna and find out if she was the one who returned the jewelry and why. He said he would do it. But in exchange, he wanted me to locate his sister, with whom he had lost contact ten years before.

"If you write down all of her information, I'll give it to Bill Pavelic," I said. "He can find anybody."

Billy did later confirm that Donna was the woman who had tossed the stolen jewelry into the Modesto Police Department lobby. Pavelic used the information Billy provided him and eventually helped him to reconnect with his sister.

Todd and Pearce were acquainted with the woman who turned in the Medinas' jewelry. They also knew the man with the 666 tattoo on his forehead. What else did they know?

According to the satanic calendar, July 1 is known as the

Night the Demon Revels. By now, it was almost 11:00 at night. My friend Brad and I decided to drive to the Woodward Reservoir campgrounds to see what was going on.

Outside the campground area we could see a huge bonfire with at least fifty to seventy-five people standing around it. The fire went into the air probably thirty-five feet. There was no one else in the area. It almost looked like a pep rally.

We parked in an area where we couldn't be seen. One man began reading to the others. We watched these people for a long time. At one point we got out of the car to check the area for vans. Finally, a lot of people in the group began to leave. We thought it was time to get out of there before they saw us. We didn't know exactly what this group was doing but thought it would be unwise to ask them.

I ended up making many more trips from Modesto to the Woodward Reservoir. The reservoir, I thought, was key, not only because the satanic group who promised a Christmas murder stayed there, but also because of another short police report I'd come across in discovery.

On March 2, 2003, at 5:49 P.M., Officer John French of the California Highway Patrol, stationed out of Modesto, reported arresting a male traveler for possession of heroin. During a search of the man's vehicle, the officer found a tape recorder. Officer French wrote in his report: "On recorder was a conversation, was something strange. A blurb where arrestee is discussing a pregnant woman and something about taking her to a reservoir. Almost sounds like he said the name Laci."

The California Highway Patrol seized the tape, then turned it over to the Modesto Police Department. There is no other reference to this tape in the discovery. I still think there should have been follow-up on this arrestee to see if he was connected with the rest of our neighborhood criminals. Specifically, did he have any connection to the group in the brown van that was staying at Woodward Reservoir? And most important, what did he know about the disappearance of Laci Peterson?

My friend Brad had to get back to his life in Oxnard, about five hours south of Modesto. I wished I could get away from the heat and hostility of the place, too.

To someone with my background, someone who grew up in Long Beach, California, and who had considerable success as a career prosecutor, at first the idea of cults sounded as outlandish to me as it did to some members of the press. But I was no longer in Southern California; I was in the Central Valley, which I soon learned was home to numerous satanic groups.

As I investigated further, I discovered that between 1999 and 2002, six other pregnant women had been reported missing and presumed dead within eighty miles of Modesto—within eighty miles of Laci Peterson.

- Dena Raley McCluskey, thirty-six, disappeared from Modesto on October 10, 1999.
- Also in October 1999, Michelle Chan of Fremont disappeared.

- Alice Sin, twenty-one, of Pinole, west of Sacramento, was reported missing on November 21, 1999. Her body was found in January 2000 in the Nevada desert.
- Angelina Joy Evans of Sacramento was last seen May 21, 2001, getting into a truck in Sacramento.
- In August 2002, the body of twenty-four-year-old Salvadoran immigrant Evelyn Hernandez washed up in San Francisco Bay. Neither the child Hernandez was carrying nor her six-year-old son, Alex, has been found.
- Rebekah Rachel Miller, thirty-three, disappeared October 15, 2002, from Modesto, twelve blocks from the Peterson home.

I was shocked by these numbers, and I was especially struck by the parallels between the Evelyn Hernandez case and that of Laci Peterson. Here we had an abduction, with the victim's personal belongings, her wallet, found in the street. A witness in the Peterson case said that he found a pair of women's sandals on the street and pointed them out to a Modesto police officer, who apparently did nothing about it. The description given by the witness matched a pair Laci owned, and Laci's pair could not be located.

Both Laci and Evelyn disappeared on satanic holy days, according to the satanic calendar, and they both ended up in the San Francisco Bay with their hands, feet, and heads missing. I began to read everything I could about satanism, satanic cults, and ritual abuse.

The rest of my time was spent reviewing the endless discovery, interviewing witnesses, and going to the jail to see Scott.

I discovered that I was in an area with a high concentration of satanic cults. Consider these words from the poem "Modesto, Land of Satan," written by a local and posted on the Internet: "Central Land Modesto, you all bear the wrath of Satan. Nothing will allow you to dissolve of this. You are under it and don't realize that Satan runs this place . . ." Even the Modesto Police Department had a special unit focused on cult activity within the city. In the 1990s, a grand jury was convened by local authorities apparently looking into the area's cult problem. In Modesto, you could open up the local phone book and find a ritual-abuse counselor. That was true for most of the surrounding cities as well.

The Children of Satan cult had an encampment in nearby Salida, a city just a couple of miles north of Modesto. Several of its members were convicted in the 1990s on murder charges. According to the charges, they murdered other cult members who were trying to leave. One of the members of the Children of Satan was quoted as saying, "Nothing is more pure than the sacrifice of a child."

I thought of the Petersons' baby and felt a chill.

The cult members were prosecuted by District Attorney Jim Brazelton, the same man in charge of the office prosecuting Scott Peterson. I am sure he would admit that cult activity in that area is a reality.

In his book *Edge of Evil: The Rise of Satanism in North*

America, Jerry Johnston estimates that thousands of victims have been killed through ritual homicides. Johnston attributes significance to the number of ritual dates during the satanic calendar that call for human sacrifice. These dates are recognized by numerous satanic groups around the world. May 1, known as the Grand Climax, and December 24, known as the High Grand Climax, are both considered days of sacrifice, according to almost all of the satanic calendars. I was beginning to think that it wasn't a coincidence that Evelyn Hernandez and Laci Peterson disappeared on those days, and that both ended up in the same bay—their hands, feet, and heads missing.

I became obsessed with reading accounts from former satanic cult members and began communicating with George Mather, a Lutheran minister who has investigated satanic incidents throughout the United States and acts as a consultant to police departments around the country. He had acquired much of his knowledge on the subject by interviewing former cult members. Most types of satanism, he said, are eclectic; therefore, they may tend to encompass many differing occult philosophies. Some groups follow a systemic philosophy of occult religion and many do not.

Mather, coauthor of *Dictionary of Cults, Sects, Religions and the Occult,* and founder and director of the New England Institute of Religious Research, said, "For all practical purposes, satanism is the worship of evil and its reaction against Christianity. It is very strange, to say the least, which makes it hard for some to believe in its existence. Yet the existence of satanism is a well-known fact. I once had a young satanist tell me that it doesn't matter what I know about his teachings or who I would tell, because it's so bizarre no one would believe me. This to some degree is true. In addition, you should be aware that it doesn't matter if one believes in the supernatural claims of the occult or not, but it is important to know that the practitioners do. Therefore they can be very dangerous. We have all seen the results of religious fanatics."

While working on the Peterson investigation, I received a letter from a woman whose daughter became involved with a satanic cult. Her daughter claimed to have seen a child sacrificed. She had to seek psychiatric counseling because of the visions she still experiences.

The daughter recalls one of the higher-up members—a priestess, she believes—wearing a hooded robe. She claimed to have seen a crying baby placed on an altar in front of the priestess, who then took what looked like a dagger and thrust it into the baby's chest. The baby stopped moving, the daughter said, and became silent.

The woman ended her letter by saying that members of her daughter's cult and other cults they associated with had moved to northern California.

I also uncovered an account from a former cult member living near Modesto. She was from Turlock, a small city just south of Modesto, and was being counseled by the Cult Awareness Project in northern California. The woman said that her involvement with satanism was due to her grandmother. As a baby, she was put on an altar and dedicated to Satan and was slated to be the cult's next high priestess, she said.

She said that she recalled going to playgrounds and luring children into vans.

"The cult members would watch from the van," she said. "They would tell me to befriend the child and not to make any mistakes."

She said that her usual method was to tell the victim that she needed to check in with her mother. When the child walked toward the satanists' van, one of the adults would grab him or her. Many of the children were taken in by the cult and would grow up within it. Others, she said, were used in rituals.

In early July, I drove back to Los Angeles to meet Mark Geragos and Bill Pavelic at the office. Since I got there a little early, I took time to read the e-mails that had piled up in the weeks I'd been gone, much of it too confidential to trust with anyone else. Strangers seemed to have no trouble tracking down my e-mail address to offer tips and hate mail alike. I received one note from a former cult member from Ohio. She wrote that her former cult would infiltrate neighborhoods, committing simultaneous burglaries and thefts in the same location.

I told Geragos about the e-mail and pointed out that there were six criminal incidents in Laci's neighborhood, all reported to the police and all occurring around the time she disappeared.

Now we had an e-mail from a former cult member who said her cult would go on sprees committing simultaneous crimes in the same neighborhood including simultaneous residential burglaries, I said. It appeared we had the same type of thing going on in our case, the same modus operandi.

After our meeting, I continued reviewing my e-mail messages. Some of them appeared to be from intelligent, educated people who had no doubt that satanists had abducted Laci as part of the Grand Climax. A former cult member from Australia claimed that he actually saw a human tortured and sacrificed as part of a ritual.

The beliefs and practices of these people seemed consistent no matter what part of the world they were from. There were just too many different accounts of sacrifice and ritual abuse told by different people all independently describing the same things. Previously, I would not have given these subjects a second thought. Now I began to believe that satanic ritual abuse really existed.

In the thirty thousand pages of material the police gave us in discovery, I found this short report written by Officer Smith.

On 01-01-03 at approximately 1600 hours, I responded to Fox Grove Park at the request of Sgt. Helton. Upon arrival I took digital photographs of a white plastic five-gallon bucket. The bucket was on its side and the contents were spilling into the river. The contents appeared to be internal organs. I took digital photographs of a second white plastic bucket that was on the bank of the river. I also photographed the contents, which appeared to be internal organs, of the second bucket.

Deputy Coroner Cline took control and custody of the buckets and contents. At the request of Sergeant Helton, I also took photographs of a black pair of jeans that was found along the riverbank.

Fox Grove Park is located outside of Modesto. One week after Laci's disappearance, two buckets were discovered containing what appeared to be internal organs. Yet there appeared to be no follow-up investigation into this matter. I had questions. Were these human organs? Was this part of some ritual? Six pregnant women disappear in the area over a three-year period, two on satanic holy days. Those two were both dismembered and found in the same bay. A wave of crimes and potential crimes occurring in Laci's quiet neighborhood started the night of December 23, ending Christmas Eve. All of the suspects came from the same part of town. Something was going on.

I was frustrated that we were denied access to the police file regarding the investigation in the Evelyn Hernandez disappearance to see if there were any other parallels with Laci's disappearance. Were any of the suspicious vehicles seen in the Peterson neighborhood the day Laci disappeared also spotted in the area where Evelyn Hernandez was last seen? Was Evelyn's neighborhood infiltrated with felons as Laci's had been the day she disappeared? We were not able to find out.

The San Francisco police and the Modesto police looked at each homicide as being unrelated. Each, they considered, was domestic in nature—meaning that they suspected a family member—and information from the two agencies was not shared. Of course, it could have been otherwise if either department desired or if the district attorney wished.

San Francisco police admitted publicly that their investigation into the Hernandez murder wasn't going anywhere. In the discovery that was given to us by the prosecution, there was a stray reference to the Evelyn Hernandez disappearance. The defense made a motion in court before Judge Al Girolami to get follow-up material on the Evelyn Hernandez investigation from the San Francisco Police Department. The San Francisco Police Department had representatives present at the hearing. They objected to the release of any of their files, claiming they were confidential. The judge denied our motion, and we were not permitted access to the Hernandez file, although we were given autopsy photographs. The photographs were incredibly similar to what I had seen in the Laci autopsy photos: a woman who had been eight months pregnant with no head, no hands, and no feet.

7

SATANIC ART,
SATANIC KILLINGS

On a cold, overcast Tuesday in July 2003, I drove to the San Francisco Bay. After checking into a cheap hotel in Richmond, I drove to the location where the bodies had been found.

From where I stood, I could see Brooks Island just offshore. Early on, Scott made a statement that on December 24 he took his small boat out of the Berkeley Marina around Fleming Point and headed toward the island. He hugged the coastline and stopped to fly-fish periodically in the bay.

The police thought that Scott took Laci out into the bay off of Brooks Island, and the media had reported the area where he had said that he was fishing. A criminal capable of abduction is also capable of planting evidence to set up someone else for the crime they committed. I needed to figure out how Laci's body could have been in the water so long if she had not been pushed out of a boat by Scott.

From where the bodies had washed ashore, you could walk along the coastline a short distance and wind up at the tip of Fleming Point. This point extends into San Francisco Bay for about a mile. I walked the entire area looking for anything of interest. Both bodies were found close to what is called the Inner Richmond Harbor. It's like a long cove located just north of Fleming Point. The wind and current conditions are much calmer compared to the middle of the San Francisco Bay.

Next, I drove out along Fleming Point, which was inaccessible by foot because of the rocks and the high tide. At the tip of the point, I discovered numerous scenes painted on plywood. There had to be ten or more of these paintings, most of them of the devil or demons. Many were depictions of people being beheaded by devil figures. One appeared to be of Jesus under a Christmas tree surrounded by red demons, as if part of a ritual. One painting was of a pregnant woman with severed hands and feet. I could hardly believe it.

I had a contact in nearby Berkeley who had grown up in the area, and I arranged to meet with him and ask him about the satanists in that area. All the way there I thought about the painting of the woman.

In high school, my contact had dated a girl who belonged to the Church of Satan, which was founded in Berkeley, California. When I asked him to tell me about them, he drove me by the church headquarters. We wanted to go inside, but the front door was locked, and the place looked closed.

He said that the satanic-looking artwork at the end of Fleming Point had been there for some time prior to Laci's murder and that it inspired all sorts of satanic fanatics to go to that spot.

"There used to be a homeless encampment out there," he told me, "but the police kicked them out."

He also said that he once saw a group of satanists from a cult called Ordo Templi Orientis—Order of the Temple of the East—out by the paintings. Dressed in black robes and hoods, these people stood in a circle while one read from a book. Ordo Templi Orientis, Temple of Set, and the Church of Satan are three of the largest satanic cults in the country. They all started here in Berkeley, he told me.

A satanic element was clearly active in Berkeley, and I was intrigued by this satanic artwork and those it was attracting to the area.

I watched a documentary film recommended to me that focused on the area of Fleming Point, known to locals as the Albany Bulb. A colony of homeless people at the end of the point had built their own structures to live in. One person had built and resided in a small castlelike structure made of boulders and rocks.

Members of that community lived there together until the police drove them out several years ago. Some had returned and lived there secretly, I was told. One man interviewed in the documentary was angry that he had been driven out. All that he had was gone, he said. Later in the film, he talked with obvious approval about the satanic artwork.

How could all of these paintings of people being beheaded go unnoticed right next to the area where Conner and Laci washed up? Across the bay from where Evelyn Hernandez washed up? Laci and Evelyn had their heads removed from their bodies, as well as their hands and feet. Many of these paintings depicted people in the same condition: heads, hands, and feet being severed from human bodies. To ignore such obvious similarities in the artwork to the condition of Laci and Evelyn's bodies was unexplainable.

My next step was to figure out what would happen if you threw a body off the end of the point, where the paintings were. I spoke to one of the divers working on the Richmond Bridge retrofitting project. He told me that during tidal changes, the current in the middle of the bay gets up to eight or nine knots.

"Divers actually have to tie themselves to the bridge when they are working," he said. He then pulled out a chart that showed the currents in the bay. The chart indicated a current flow from the top of the point toward the direction of the Inner Richmond Harbor, where the bodies were found.

"The current from the end of Fleming Point to the Inner Richmond Harbor is much different. It's a much slower current. It runs right here," he said, pointing on the map to the area where Laci and Conner washed up.

Now I knew that the weighted bodies could have easily been thrown from the end of Fleming Point. Over time, the slow current would have pushed them along the bottom to the

Inner Richmond Harbor, where extremely high tides and ocean swells would eventually wash them ashore. This could explain why Laci's body was in the water so long. She was getting pushed slowly down-current. In my opinion, it appeared the baby had been protected inside the pallet bag.

Still amazed and disgusted by the artwork I'd found, I was encouraged by how well the facts were developing in my investigation. And I was ready to go back to Modesto.

ANOTHER MURDER

On my way back to Modesto, I got a call from my brother, who told me the media was reporting a possible satanic killing. The man who'd committed the crime was from Berkeley, my brother said.

In June 2003, Perry Monroe of Alameda, California—the town next to Berkeley—checked into the Hacienda Hotel, outside of Boulder City, Nevada. This was the summer solstice, a day of death ritual, according to the satanic calendar. Monroe called a chambermaid up for towels in the afternoon at or around the time of the summer solstice. When she delivered them, he killed her.

The following Monday morning, a woman walking her dog discovered human body parts in the fishing pond at Veterans' Memorial Park in Boulder City. Police investigators found a woman's torso—no head, no hands, no feet. The body was that of the maid, Ladonna Milam. That Tuesday, Monroe was arrested in Fresno, California; his victim's hands, feet, and head were recovered from his car.

We attempted to speak to Monroe after his arrest, while he was awaiting extradition in the Fresno County Jail. Fresno, also in the central San Joaquin Valley, is located only a few hours from Modesto.

Monroe would not speak to us. Although the media reported that he was a possible satanist, we couldn't find any solid proof of that.

I kept thinking about the timing of what appeared to be a premeditated ambush. Why in the afternoon during the summer solstice, a ritual day? Was this another coincidence, I thought, or a connection to the Hernandez and Laci Peterson murders?

Did the removal of the hands, feet, and heads have religious significance? The alleged satanist, Perry Monroe, was still in possession of his victim's hands, feet, and head. Why? Was he taking them back to the Berkeley area? Was somebody holding on to Laci's and Evelyn's missing hands and feet the same way Perry Monroe had held on to the body parts of his victim?

Was there a group of fanatics in this area responsible for these horrible murders occurring on satanic holy days?

In June 2003, a man from Yolo County, just north of Modesto, threw severed human hands and feet into a trash Dumpster. As soon as I heard about the incident, I traveled there to speak to the Yolo County coroner. The coroner told me that they were going to attempt to identify the people from whom the body parts were taken. Some appeared to be female hands, she said, and they were going to do a DNA comparison with Laci. Weeks went by, and finally the coroner said that the tests could not be conducted because their machine was down.

I then spoke to our religion expert, George Mather, about the missing body parts in Laci's and Evelyn's cases and the significance to a satanist of keeping possession of a victim's body parts. Mather said that mutilation is very important, and missing body parts are to be expected in a satanic rite. Fingers, toes, sexual organs, arms, legs, hair, head, and heart are frequently removed. Mather also told me about a satanist he interviewed who had kept preserved human fingers in a jar. According to the *Dictionary of Mysticism and the Occult* by Nevill Drury, even body fat is sometimes used in sacrifices and rituals.

While I was living in Modesto, I became friends with Jenny M——, a resident who was very much against the satanic underworld she said existed in her city. She had originally contacted the Peterson family before contacting me. Her former boyfriend, she told me, who lived just outside the airport district in Modesto, was a satanist. Regarding the disappearance of Laci Peterson, she said, "He is either responsible or knows something."

One day Jenny telephoned me and asked if I would meet her by the park where Laci was last seen. I did, and she gave me a small bag of what she claimed were human bones she had taken from her former boyfriend. I then gave that bag of bones to Mark Geragos. I don't know if tests were ever run on them.

Although my contact Billy J——, the ex-husband of one of the women in the brown van, said he thought Jenny's boyfriend's name sounded familiar, I was never able to connect this man with any of the criminal element operating in Laci's neighborhood when she disappeared.

The preliminary hearing was about to start. We couldn't afford to spend too much time on all of the possible alternative theories developed during my investigation at the expense of not preparing to defend against the prosecution's case. But in my opinion, there was too much doubt concerning Scott's guilt and several leads suggesting Laci may have been abducted and murdered.

8

AMBER FREY: A MOTIVE FOR MURDER?

Few aspects of the Peterson murder trial have been as heavily publicized as Amber Frey. "Mistress" was the media label for her, but my dictionary defines the term as "a woman other than his wife with whom a married man has a continuing sexual relationship." I don't think Amber Frey qualifies.

When it comes to Amber, you have two camps, and neither is neutral. In one camp, she is the heroine who brought about Scott Peterson's downfall by having the courage to come forward. In another, she is tabloid fodder, a wannabe actress/model who's been around the block and fell too soon for yet one more married man. I don't see her as either.

Amber Frey, as we know her, is the unlikely but possible motive for those looking for a reason to prove that Scott Peterson killed his wife and unborn child. The media Amber has little to do with the real Amber, who was simply another woman with whom Scott Peterson had sex after he was married.

I can't defend his behavior in that regard. Nor am I going to bash Amber Frey, as others have. It could not have been easy for her to come forward once she realized that the *public* Scott Peterson was *her* Scott Peterson.

I believe that Scott Peterson considered Amber Frey another in a series of sexual relationships in which he engaged behind Laci's back. I don't think that Peterson was in love with Amber or ever had been. Not that he didn't care about her; I think on some level he cared about Amber and all the women with whom he'd had sexual encounters.

The way she was introduced to the media and the public at a police press conference made her appear more important than she was. Here, in the midst of the mystery surrounding Laci's disappearance, was a young, single woman who could prove that Scott Peterson was an unfaithful husband. But nothing more. To the public, however, and the media, she represented the key witness for the prosecution and possibly a motive for murder.

BEFORE GLORIA ALLRED, AFTER GLORIA ALLRED

In May, attorney Gloria Allred announced that she was representing Amber Frey. This alone brought even more media attention to the case because of Ms. Allred's celebrity status.

"It will be for the district attorney to make the decision as to what role [Amber] will play in the prosecution of the case," Allred said. "I will say that it's my opinion what she has to say in testimony is very important to the case."

When we first saw Gloria Allred on our way to court, Mark immediately went up and hugged her, and they talked for ten or fifteen minutes.

At some point, Allred made a statement to the press that Mark thought violated the gag order. He insisted on a hearing. That hearing lasted all morning, and Mark was rude to her, at one point referring to Allred in court as "a bad *Saturday Night Live* skit."

Allred did not respond, leaving that to someone else from her law firm. As I sat there, I couldn't help thinking about how the entire morning's hearing had nothing to do with Scott Peterson. I don't believe his name was brought up once that day.

MOTIVE FOR MURDER

I must admit that while I was involved in the investigation of the case, I completely underestimated the impact Amber Frey would have on the eventual outcome. She was introduced to the case regarding the issue of motive; that is, to assert Scott would have had a reason to murder his wife and unborn child so that he could be with Amber. It seemed to me that would be relatively easy to refute, since Amber was less attractive than Laci, had a child of her own, and the relationship with Scott was of a relatively short duration. Geragos seemed to share this evaluation in his address to the jury:

> *In June when they made their opening statement, do you remember what the theory was of this case then? The theory of this then was it was Amber. And the theory of this case was that he had met Amber on November 20th, and when he met Amber on November 20th, two days later he was so taken with Amber that he planned this trip, or he told her he was going to go out of town. And guess what happened during the course of this case? It became apparent to anyone sitting here, including them, when Amber testified—and I have a lot to say about Amber—but clearly Amber was not the motive. Nobody was going to kill Laci Peterson and their child for Amber Frey. I mean, that's—that's a given. After seeing her, after hearing her testify, that was not going to happen.*

Even if we dismiss the premise that Amber provided a motive for Scott to murder his wife and unborn child, the revelation of this affair could still have done sufficient damage to Scott to weigh heavily in the verdict against him. And in fact, the revelation of his infidelity may well have been a deciding factor in his conviction.

"While they were looking for his wife and son, he was romancing his girlfriend. It doesn't make sense. It doesn't make sense at all," said jury foreman Steve Cardosi at a press conference after the trial.

Laci's family immediately turned against Scott publicly. He was shown to be a scoundrel and a liar. An irony here is that though Amber very likely did not prove to be a motive, exposing her involvement with him further damaged the perception of his character and led to the revelation of his other sexual encounters. The police conducted an extensive investigation into Scott's past and quickly learned that this was not his only sexual dalliance since his marriage to Laci. All of this surfaced only because of the issue of motive, which it probably did not establish.

No one can quarrel with Amber's actions in revealing her relationship with Scott when she discovered that he was under investigation regarding the murder of his wife. It was the only proper thing for her to do under the circumstances. She is to be given credit for exposing what had to be an embarrassment for her. This episode was what it was for Scott, and there was nothing that could be done about it. With twenty-twenty hindsight, it probably should have rested there.

At the time, however, we felt we had to do whatever we could to show that Amber was not and could not have ever provided a motive for murder. Our initial inquiry regarding Amber Frey led us to her sister, Ava Frey.

Ava Frey lived in Modesto, not far from the Peterson house. We met at the Doubletree in Modesto. Ava carried a tiny poodle, which she held throughout the interview. Much of what she told me about her sister seemed motivated by what was then a contentious relationship between them.

Ava told me that she could name several relationships in which Amber fell in love with a man after only knowing the man for a short period of time. When Amber began dating Peterson, Ava told their mother that Amber was once again falling head over heels for somebody she hardly knew. She and her mother discussed the probability of Peterson being married, since he never seemed to be around. Peterson was not the first married man with whom Amber had been involved, and they did not want to see that happen again.

Did Amber know that Scott was married? According to Ava, the family was suspicious enough that they hired an investigator after Amber began seeing him. I don't know whether the statement made by Ava was true; I heard nothing else about it. What I do know is that when Amber put a photo of Peterson and herself in her Christmas cards after dating him only three times, her family was concerned that she would get hurt falling yet again for another unavailable man. The circulation of this picture of a grinning Scott Peterson with another woman at a party while his lovely, pregnant wife had spent that evening attending a party alone had to have a devastating effect on potential jurors.

Regardless of whether or not Amber suspected that Peterson was married, on December 29 she learned from her friend

Richard Byrd, a Fresno homicide detective, that Scott was a suspect in his wife's disappearance. She didn't call Peterson and ask for an explanation; she called the Modesto police.

Ava also said that her sister refused to let her look at the script the police had given her for use in taping Scott's telephone calls at their request. In these calls, Scott consistently denied involvement with Laci's disappearance. She told me that Amber said that there were instances when she taped Scott and didn't give the tapes to the police.

I'm not going to go into all of the charges Ava made against her sister, since most of them do not pertain to the Peterson case. Once the affair itself was established, it did not advance the case of Peterson to discredit or demean Amber Frey any more than it would have helped Bill Clinton to attack the morality of Monica Lewinsky.

Amber had a history of making poor decisions where men were concerned. Scott was another poor decision. It was a poor decision for each of them. Perhaps a fatal one for Scott Peterson.

There is nothing that I saw, however, that indicates that Scott's extramarital affairs impacted upon his relationship with his wife. All of Scott and Laci's friends with whom I spoke confirmed that he treated Laci extremely well: standing up when she entered a room, obeying her requests to take out the garbage, never interrupting her. No one ever heard him raise his voice to her. They described the couple as being like "best friends."

On their first date, in 1994, Scott took Laci deep-sea fishing. After leaving California Polytechnic State University at San

Luis Obispo, Scott broke with his father's manufacturing busi-ness so that he and Laci could open a restaurant and buy a win-ery. This was after his first extramarital affair, which police reports indicate Laci knew about, but his focus appeared to be Laci. Just as important, there was no report from any of the women who had relationships with Peterson that he had ever been violent or displayed any anger toward them. Nor was there any evidence in the police's exhaustive investigations into the issue that Scott had ever been violent in his treatment of Laci.

I learned nothing in my investigation that indicated to me that Scott's interest in Amber Frey was anything but transitory.

In his summation to the jury, Mark Geragos said that he thought Scott was honest in his interview with Diane Sawyer when he said that he respected Amber and that he continued to call Amber after their relationship was revealed because he wanted her to believe he was innocent while others were turn-ing against him. He described their relationship as a friendship.

Instead of focusing so much on Amber Frey's relationship to the case, the real effort should have been on getting the case to a preliminary hearing to determine if there was sufficient evidence to hold Peterson for trial. California law requires that a hearing be held within ten days after a defendant has pleaded not guilty to the charges against him. This is to prevent lengthy pretrial incarceration for someone in a custodial situa-tion, as Scott was, or to assure a reasonably prompt resolution, if appropriate, for those accused of crimes whether in or out of custody.

This right can be waived by the defendant, and Scott reluctantly agreed to continuances because of delays in our defense team's being provided with much of the discovery materials.

In my opinion, it would have been more appropriate to proceed to the preliminary hearing and put on the stand our eyewitnesses who would testify they saw a woman identified as Laci Peterson walking a dog on December 24. This could have refuted the prosecution's entire case. The testimony of one of the witnesses, elderly neighbor Vivian Mitchell, has been lost forever because of her death. If there is ever a retrial of this case, it will be a question then if the others are still available. If they had testified at the preliminary hearing, their testimony would have been preserved even if they were later unavailable.

Scott remained confident that the entire matter would be straightened out.

"They won't convict me, because I didn't do it," he told me.

He did not know that this was not always enough.

9

THE VICTIMS

The bodies of Laci and Conner were recovered separately. The baby was discovered washed up on shore on April 13, 2003, and Laci was found the next day. It was not until August 2003 that our two forensic experts, Drs. Henry Lee and Cyril Wecht, examined the remains.

I was never clear as to the reason for this delay and do not know if an earlier examination would have been any more revealing, but the condition of the physical remains by that time left insufficient evidence for any scientific conclusions as to the cause of the deaths.

Both of these gentlemen were familiar faces on court-related television talk shows and had national reputations. Both had testified in celebrated cases in the past and were deservedly highly regarded.

Neither was used as a witness at the trial. By that time I was no longer on the case, and that is a decision that can only be made by the trial lawyer. They had both spoken about the case on television prior to being retained, and it may have been something said in those earlier interviews that was the determining factor.

It is well known by trial lawyers that experts can generally be found for either side of an issue within their field of expertise. It is not only superior qualifications that may affect the jury's acceptance of an expert's testimony; factors such as how articulate, personable, and even how charismatic they are may instead carry the day. It is enough to say that both of these gentlemen were well qualified and favorites of trial lawyers.

I picked up Lee and Wecht at San Francisco International Airport. We escaped the television news people and drove to our Contra Costa hotel from there. On the way, I brought them up to date on the case and the results of my investigation. Both men seemed very receptive to what I said. They already appeared to have questions about the prosecution's case from what they had heard on television regarding the lack of physical evidence.

Geragos and Bill Pavelic met us at the hotel. On the conference room's big-screen television, we displayed the slides the district attorney gave us of Laci and the baby. When the photograph of Conner's body was shown, Cyril Wecht especially looked visibly shocked. He got out of his chair and stood a few feet from the screen.

"They sure misrepresented this to me," he said finally. I assumed he was referring to the information he had previously relied upon when going on television. Looking now at this picture of the baby with objects attached to him appeared to put Dr. Wecht into a state of deep thought. After a long pause, he said, "Do you think we can get one of these cult members to talk?"

Just like that! I thought. One look at the photo! This did not look like the work of an angry husband. It looked like someone had handled the baby outside the womb. How else could you explain these items attached to the baby? How could you explain the weights? And how else could you explain that smell in the bag?

Mark's confidence grew by the moment. He turned to the man running the projector, handed him a dollar, and said, "Hey, get me a Diet Coke, will you?"

After the projectionist had left, we sat around waiting, and Wecht continued to comment about cults and the possibility of getting a cult member to come forward. Because so little remained of Laci's body, the expert opinion was that the baby could not have been protected inside her body. The other explanation was that the baby had recently been inside the pallet cover bag that washed up near the bodies. That could explain why the baby's corpse did not decompose or get eaten by sea life.

At trial, a police officer testified that this bag smelled like decaying human flesh. This fact was not written in any police report that I had read.

Next to this pallet cover bag were metal pipes that also had duct tape wrapped around them. It seemed that this physical evidence supported the theory that the baby was in the bag and those pipes may have been used as weights to sink the body.

The metal pipes with duct tape, the pallet cover bag with duct tape, the body of Laci Peterson with duct tape, and the body of Conner Peterson all washed up in the same general location at the same time. They appear to be connected.

The next morning we went to the coroner's office to view the remains in person. Representatives from the district attorney's office were also present. We put on plastic hats and covered our noses with masks.

We entered a small examining room adjoining a second room containing a walk-in freezer. Wecht walked right in without a mask, and I figured that maybe in time one got used to the grisly realities of such a job. I knew that I never would.

They brought out Laci first. Wecht began examining her remains while Pavelic displayed on his laptop the photo of the baby with the nooselike plastic tape around his neck and chest, and the material on his ear. Pavelic positioned his computer near the middle of the room so everyone could see it. As I watched the gruesome scene of which I was now a part, I thought to myself: Whoever did this to poor Laci was a monster. I was now more obsessed than ever with finding out what really happened to her.

After the examination, I asked Wecht if there was any evidence indicating that Laci's feet had been removed using a tool or if they'd been broken away. He said that she was too badly decomposed and there was not enough of her remaining to make a determination. I thought again of the tape on the pallet bag that the officer said smelled like human remains and the apparent attached weights.

I wanted to know if there was any evidence indicating that her limbs were attached to anchors. Wecht said no, there wasn't enough left of Laci's body to make that determination either.

They put her remains into a bag and put the bag back into the freezer.

I continued to speculate about how much her body had deteriorated and how the coroner concluded that there was no deterioration of the baby.

Now we were going to see for ourselves.

The baby was carefully brought out and placed on a table. He looked different from the photos. His body had shrunk, and in the bright light of the room I could see that he did not look fully developed. His eyes were closed, and I immediately noticed the mark on the side of his face.

Months after he was found, what appeared to be an adhesive mark was still visible. I had seen photos with and without the material on the ear and thought I knew what the mark was. I said, "We've got to get a sample of the material along the side of his face."

Such a sample might have been key to the issue of whether that was tape or seaweed holding down the baby's ear. I knew that that factual determination would go a long way in proving the baby was handled outside of Laci's body. Unfortunately, we didn't get a sample, and the baby's body has since been cremated, so that evidence could never be presented to the jury.

Geragos wanted to develop his theory that the baby was born alive. "You need someone who specializes in that area," Wecht said to Geragos after the examination.

I will never forget how it felt to see the bodies of Laci and Conner Peterson. Nothing I could say would adequately describe the horror and sense of loss. I know that from that moment, if not before, I wasn't just working as a defense attorney. I was working for Laci, to find out who did this to her and bring the murderer to justice.

We drove back to Modesto, and I gave Lee and Wecht a tour of the Petersons' neighborhood. We then stopped at the home of Vivian Mitchell, the elderly woman who said that she was positive she saw Laci on the morning of December 24. Mrs. Mitchell was happy to recount her story for the visitors. When I glanced over at Wecht and Lee, I noticed that both of them were starting to look very tired.

On the way back to the airport, we stopped in the area where the bodies were found. Henry Lee took photos and discussed possible theories, including the possibility of the bodies being planted.

The bodies of Laci and Conner washed up a day apart during a period of extremely high tides and large ocean swells. On the spot where Laci was found, I could see across the bay to where Evelyn Hernandez's body was found.

"The hands, feet, and heads of these women were never recovered?" Henry asked.

"That's correct," I said.

"Those body parts would all float to the surface in saltwater," he said.

It would be difficult to explain why those body parts were separated from the bodies and why they were never found.

We were supposed to meet the district attorney at the California State Department of Justice in Ripon so that our experts could look at evidence relating to the case being kept there, but no representative from the DA's office showed up. We had prearranged this meeting with the district attorney's office knowing our experts were in town for only one day. But Lee and Wecht were unable to get into the Department of Justice crime lab as had been scheduled. Our experts never got to look at the evidence they had.

In my experience, most lawyers will treat each other cordially through the pretrial and discovery stages of a case. This was something different.

I dropped Lee and Wecht off at the San Francisco airport. It had been a long day, and I knew a San Francisco hotel room wouldn't be an option. I would have to drive all the way back to Modesto again.

I was on my way back to my sleeping quarters above the J Street Café when I received a call from Geragos. He was still focused on the idea that the baby was born alive and lived past the twenty-fourth, when police had started tailing Scott. He wanted me to stop in Contra Costa County, where the bodies were being kept, to set up an MRI for the Peterson baby.

I told him that I didn't see how we could make it happen, that it would be difficult to find anyone who would allow us to use their MRI equipment for a dead baby. We really clashed on the phone, and I sensed the tension between us becoming something I could no longer laugh off or ignore.

Still, I tried for him. I contacted numerous state facilities only to find that I was correct. It was unprecedented, I was told. No facility was going to allow us to put a dead baby in its million-dollar MRI machine.

Geragos eventually got a radiologist from the hospital where his father-in-law worked to try and determine the baby's age using an MRI. We returned to Contra Costa and looked at the baby's body again for the purpose of Mark's getting measurements to prove his theory.

We had very knowledgeable experts in Lee and Wecht, but I feared that we hadn't learned enough to be able to discover what really happened to Laci and Conner. For the first time, I wondered if we ever would.

10

A NEW DEFENSE TEAM?

Scott became increasingly frustrated by what he perceived as a lack of progress on the defense team's part. I could understand that. He wanted to move forward with the case. He adamantly declared his innocence. He was exhausted, frustrated, and tired of being locked up.

"Let's talk to other lawyers," he told me, "but I want you to stay on the case."

Enter Howrey, Simon, Arnold, and White.

Howrey, Simon, Arnold, and White is, by most standards, a silk-stocking law firm. Founded as Howrey and Simon in Washington, D.C., in 1956, it built its reputation representing numerous blue-ribbon clients. Later they opened a Los Angeles office with the acquisition of two local midlevel litigators, Stephen Miller and Thomas Nolan.

My father, a retired lawyer, had considered Miller a friend for a number of years. They shared numerous professional contacts and were members of the same golf club. Upon learning of my involvement in the Peterson case, Miller expressed considerable interest, particularly when he learned from my father that Scott was considering a change of attorneys.

I had already suggested my first choice for replacement lawyers to Scott: a Los Angeles criminal-law firm with extensive state criminal experience and—particularly important—death penalty court experience. Unfortunately, that firm declined due to financial concerns.

Miller let it be known that he would like to pursue his interest by meeting with the Peterson family. From the outset, I was skeptical. What motivated this aggressive behavior, I wondered? Why would this firm have any interest in the Peterson case?

There can be no doubt that Howrey had some very capable and experienced lawyers in such areas as antitrust, commercial litigation, and intellectual property matters. These specialties, however, are far removed from the rough-and-tumble California criminal courts with daily crime and lots of activity. A few of the Howrey lawyers had handled white-collar criminal cases in the U.S. District Court, and that was about the extent of it. Although Miller had handled some of those cases in the past, he'd lost his last trial about twelve years earlier, and to my knowledge, hadn't had a jury trial since.

Another reason I feared that the firm might be out of its area of expertise is the fact that federal courts and state courts are not only separated geographically but also represent two completely different judicial systems, both protective of their own processes. They have their own rules of procedure, which cover all pretrial matters, as well as trials, rules of evidence, and posttrial and appellate proceedings. State crimes are defined primarily in the California Penal Code, while federal crimes are contained in the United States Code. California has its own evidence codes, while the federal courts follow the Federal Rules of Evidence. Questions of law, other than constitutional issues, are not binding by one court upon the other. In other words, a federal practitioner may be ill-prepared for a state practice and vice versa. Despite their advertisements in *Forbes* magazine and the *Wall Street Journal,* Miller, Nolan, and Howrey, Simon, Arnold, and White were largely unknown in California's criminal courts, where Scott Peterson's fate was to be determined.

I was concerned by their lack of experience in an arena that demanded hard-earned knowledge. However, I agreed with Scott that it might be a good idea to talk to other lawyers, and I arranged the meeting that Miller had requested.

COURTING THE CASE

We met in Howrey's downtown office in a large, impressive conference room. Jackie and Lee Peterson were accompanied by Scott's sister and brother, and Miller had requested that my father attend. That was fine with me. My father was very well known in both state and federal courts and tried many high-profile cases in his career. His book *West's California Criminal Law* is still in print and is used by many lawyers in the state. He is known by defense attorneys and prosecutors alike for his high ethical standards. In the book *Deadly Blessings*, the author Richard J. Brenneman gives this description of my father: "Douglas Dalton, Esq., perhaps Los Angeles's most esteemed criminal defense attorney . . . With his craggy, careworn features, dark hair and lanky build, there is something Lincoln-esque about him, an air that generates attention and respect in the courtroom." He was by far the best-known lawyer to attend the meeting and the only one with a national reputation.

I was glad Miller had talked him into going that day. We could use the benefit of his judgment, I thought, and he agreed to attend because of my strong feelings that someone else had murdered Laci Peterson.

The meeting was not at all what I had expected. In addition to Miller, three other Howrey lawyers, including Tom Nolan, the Los Angeles office's managing partner, showed up.

Miller is a short, heavyset man approaching seventy, with a flushed face and an effusive personality. Nolan is a humorless, balding man who had followed Miller through several law firms but now had overtaken him as managing partner.

To my surprise, Nolan promptly launched into a lengthy presentation regarding the firm's many qualities, resources, and successes. In his soft monotone, he introduced each Howrey lawyer amid flattering descriptions of each one's achievements and abilities.

This firm generally represented Fortune 500 clients, he told us, in an obvious effort to impress the Petersons. I had not expected Nolan to even be present, much less to provide a presentation in the nature of a sales pitch. Perhaps this was felt necessary, since the Petersons had never heard of Tom Nolan, Stephen Miller, *or* Howrey, Simon, Arnold, and White.

Using such marketing techniques to acquire clients is not unusual in present-day practices, but such practices are looked upon with disdain by many firms. Many of us still stick to the time-honored belief that the lawyer should interview the client, instead of the other way around. Not so that day.

No confidential attorney-client communications took place. The only real substance to the meeting as far as the actual case was concerned consisted of my presenting to the group some of the discovery material that had been turned over by the prosecution.

The Petersons had already been briefed on all of that information, and I shared it as much for the benefit of Howrey, Simon as anything. If they were really interested in the case, they needed to know what we had found out thus far. I kept the presentation neutral. I didn't want to appear as if I were trying to sell them on the facts of the case.

They were especially interested in the prior abduction in the brown van, the burglaries, the white van, and the fact that Laci had been seen by numerous witnesses. When I showed them the photo of baby Conner with the items attached to him, I could see that it affected them.

As the meeting progressed, I came to realize that they had followed the case closely. They asked questions about evidence that didn't exist, such as the blood on the mop and the infamous, nonexistent anchors.

I had a wife and two small children at home, and I wanted to continue trying to get to the bottom of what had happened to Laci Peterson. So when the managing partner offered to invest resources into the case and to give me a lucrative position of counsel to the firm, I accepted.

I then met with the Petersons in a separate room. They had a lot of questions about the new firm. They wanted to make sure my dad and I would be involved. They also wanted to make sure these lawyers knew what they were doing. Miller's main contribution that Saturday consisted of preparing a retainer agreement and a substitution-of-attorneys form (which he needed help to prepare for the state court), arranging for a van to transport a team of lawyers to Modesto, and—most telling—putting out a press release announcing that Howrey, and notably Miller, were coming in to take over the world's most celebrated case. My father had agreed to assist without a fee but insisted that his name not be used in the press release. He felt a press release sent the wrong message and served no purpose other than publicity. He preferred no publicity and would help solely because of the serious questions as to Scott's guilt.

This case the Howrey attorneys were flirting with was the

most serious kind of case that a lawyer could undertake. It required utmost dedication and singular purpose in the defense. Personal ambitions and interest could play no part.

I was concerned that the appeal of this case was the fact that it looked like a winner and would receive substantial publicity. This could be very attractive in achieving a reputation as a trial-law firm.

I knew that my father shared my feelings. Having served with a nonprofit entity that worked with the California Supreme Court to provide lawyers for death penalty conviction appeals, he knew well how frequently the issue of ineffective counsel was raised on appeal. He insisted that a lawyer with death penalty experience be added to the defense team. Miller agreed, somewhat reluctantly in my opinion.

I left the Howrey, Simon offices that day thinking that maybe the Peterson case would get better treatment from these lawyers, but I wasn't sure just how. At least they had the financial resources that we needed to prepare the strongest defense.

SECOND CHANCE FOR GERAGOS

Although Mark Geragos had not been invited to the meeting between Howrey and the Petersons, he soon learned what was taking place. He was told that I would be working with Howrey, Simon, Arnold, and White. He immediately flew to the Modesto jail to meet with Peterson. He told him that substituting this law firm was a mistake. At that meeting, Peterson decided to let Geragos remain as counsel.

I felt helpless. No one was getting any closer to finding Laci Peterson's killer. The preliminary hearing was scheduled for the following month. I might be off the case, but it wasn't out of my system, not even close.

11

THE TRIAL

Although I was no longer involved in the defense, I was convinced that I had discovered enough evidence—specifically witnesses who saw Laci the morning of December 24 after Scott had left the house—to refute the prosecution's case. I had interviewed these witnesses and I believed them.

When the trial began on June 1, 2004, the prosecution did not seem to have a set theory on when the murder occurred, where the murder occurred, or how the murder occurred. They began with the theory that Scott killed Laci on the night of the twenty-third, a so-called soft kill, using a combination of drugs to knock Laci out. Then, they surmised, he strangled her.

The theory that it occurred on the twenty-third was based

on a statement by Laci's half-sister, Amy Rocha, that Laci came to Amy's workplace, Salon Salon, wearing tan pants the evening of the twenty-third, which could be proven by the Salon Salon security videotape. Since Laci's remains were discovered clad in light-colored pants, the prosecution concluded they were the same pants she was wearing the night of December 23. Therefore, that's when Scott Peterson killed her.

Throughout the trial, the prosecution stated several times that Laci had been found wearing the same clothes from December 23. It seemed that was the original theory the police and prosecution proceeded on. Then their theory developed a problem.

Amy identified the pants that Laci had on when she last saw her on December 23; they were in Laci's closet. That was a blow to their theory.

Another problem for the prosecution during the trial was that a police computer expert found that someone had accessed Laci's computer on the morning of December 24, using Laci's password, "Sunflower."

Lydell Wall of the Stanislaus County Sheriff's Department returning to the stand for cross-examination on August 25, 2004, testified that someone used the Petersons' home computer to search shopping Web sites for a sunflower umbrella stand and a scarf on December 24, 2002, between 8:40 A.M. and 8:45 A.M.

"Who was the person who logged on at 8:40 A.M.?" Geragos asked.

Wall said authorities never asked him to determine exactly who used the home computer that morning. I believe that person more than likely was Laci.

We next heard that when talking to the police, Scott said that he and Laci had been watching Martha Stewart's cooking show on television the morning of December 24 before he left the house. Thinking that Scott was trying to fabricate an alibi, Detective Brocchini asked him what the show was about.

Scott said meringue.

Brocchini pulled the tapes of *Martha Stewart Living* and noticed that meringue was talked about on the December 23 show. Based on this, he believed that Peterson made up what happened on the December 24 show.

But on the twenty-fourth, Martha Stewart did mention meringue again. She mentioned meringue on *both* shows. The prosecution did not learn of this until it was pointed out by the defense.

During the trial, Scott and Laci's maid testified that she had been there on the twenty-third, cleaning house. She said that she had put everything away in the bathroom; yet when the police got to the house on the twenty-fourth, they took pictures inside, and Laci's hairbrush and curling iron were on the bathroom vanity.

She would have had no need for them on the twenty-third, as Laci's sister had styled her hair at the salon. Amy said that she was teaching Laci how to style her hair into a flip and that the curling iron was necessary. Laci had planned on wearing her hair in that style for the Christmas Eve party they were going to have with their family.

It is consistent from the evidence that Laci woke up the morning of the twenty-fourth, styled her hair, and did the computer research for purchasing an umbrella stand.

After these developments, the prosecution apparently changed its theory at midtrial. The prosecution usually files charges based on a theory of guilt it has reached after a review of the facts in the case and the interviews of witnesses. It is rare to see prosecutors changing their theory of the crime midtrial because testimony, for which they were not prepared, was elicited from their own witnesses.

The prosecution said to the jury in closing arguments that the murder could have been on the twenty-third *or* the twenty-fourth. After hearing all of the testimony, they now appeared unsure.

ATTACKING PROSECUTION THEORIES

Part of the testimony during the trial helped explain away a lot of the misconceptions surrounding the murder.

First was the suspicion over Scott Peterson going fishing the day before Christmas and the purchase of a two-day fishing license. A witness from Big 5 Sporting Goods testified that two-day licenses were all that they had because it was the end of the year.

Records showed that Scott purchased two-day passes for August 30 and 31 of that year, one in the year 2000, and a year-long pass in 1994. He'd fished from the time that he was three years old and owned numerous small boats, as had his family. The family had a second home near a lake where Scott first learned to fish.

At trial, a witness named Mary Anna Felix testified that Laci told her that Scott enjoyed fishing in Monterey, and he also fished in the Sacramento San Joaquin Delta area. Laci knew Scott liked to ocean fish. He even designed Conner's nursery with a nautical theme, including a border with a boy fishing from a boat.

Peterson left his warehouse to go fishing at 11:00 A.M. on December 24, 2002. The media had frequently reported that Peterson went fishing on Christmas Eve. During his opening statement, Geragos addressed this issue:

"You have heard this so many times that he went fishing on Christmas Eve. Who goes fishing Christmas Eve with an eight-month-pregnant wife? He didn't go fishing Christmas Eve. Let's make that perfectly clear. He went fishing in the morning. He left the house sometime between nine-thirty and ten o'clock. He had plans—and everybody will tell you this—to be back by four o'clock. And he was, in fact, back by four o'clock. They had plans that evening to go over to Sharon's house for Christmas Eve."

Another problematic theory involved the prosecution's claim that Laci was not walking because of her advanced pregnancy. The Petersons' maid testified that Laci did indeed go on walks. She also testified that on the morning of December 23, Laci carried her own groceries from the car into the house.

Furthermore, Laci had reported to her doctor that she was walking in order to reduce the swelling in her ankles.

The prosecution's theory on a December 23 murder lost even more credibility with the following new development from the trial testimony: Apparently the police were not aware that Scott had invited Amy, Laci's half-sister, over to Scott and Laci's home the night of the twenty-third. The evidence brought out at trial established that Amy went to Scott and Laci's, ate pizza, and watched a video with the two of them.

The strand of hair that Brocchini claimed to have found in Scott's boat could have sealed Scott's fate. The theory was that Laci had never been near the boat and did not even know of its existence. If it could then be established that the hair came from Laci and it was discovered in the boat, it would have suggested the body was placed in the boat and taken to the place of disposal.

However, a problem arose with this piece of the puzzle. The same witness Pavelic and I interviewed told Brocchini that a few days before Laci's disappearance, Laci asked to use the witness's nearby bathroom because Scott had his work products stacked all over his warehouse, and it was difficult to get to the bathroom. The witness said that she told the police what she told us, yet there was never a report filed.

During the trial, Brocchini admitted that they had talked to her, but it did not appear in a report. Based on everything else they did, it seems to me that the police didn't want to hear what the witness had to say because it didn't support their theory that Scott Peterson was guilty.

What the witness observed, of course, could explain the hair in the boat: Laci had been in the warehouse while the boat was there.

This witness's statement qualifies as exculpatory evidence—that is, it tends to exculpate, or exonerate, the accused. Every trained policeman in the United States knows or should know of the 1963 U.S. Supreme Court ruling of *Brady v. Maryland,* which has come to be referred to as "the Brady Doctrine." The Los Angeles District Attorney's Office has a special "Brady" unit to make sure all exculpatory evidence is provided to defendants.

Under Brady, it is the duty of police to disclose possible exculpatory evidence to defendants, and that the failure to do so is a violation of the defendant's right to due process of law.

A Supreme Court ruling such as this has no meaning if the police don't know about it or choose to ignore it by not reporting it. How did Detective Brocchini deal with the problem? He took it out of his report! This was his testimony:

> Geragos: Can you tell me how that particular piece of information got excised out of your police report?
>
> Brocchini: I excised it.
>
> Geragos: You did?
>
> Brocchini: I guess I did.

In the trial of a criminal case the role of the defense lawyer is to do what he can to discredit the case in chief of the prosecution. Geragos did a good job in that regard, and many observers were asking, "Is that all there is?"

Unfortunately, what the defense presented was not as successful. This was the chance to put on affirmative evidence of Scott's innocence. For reasons unknown to me, none of the eyewitnesses from the neighborhood who reported seeing Laci were presented to the jury by the defense. I had regarded this as the strongest evidence the defense had.

Although some of this was brought out in trial by the defense through the cross-examination of the police officers, the judge limited how the jury could interpret the evidence. Here is the judge's ruling on the issue:

> *I want to clear up something. Remember yesterday there was an objection by the prosecutor? This information now that this officer's receiving from these people is not being offered for the truth of that information. It's been offered to this officer to explain his conduct, what did he do.*
>
> *So if somebody says I saw A, B, and C, it's not coming in to prove that person saw A, B and C, but it's coming in to show this was what he was told and what did he do about it, okay?*

In other words, it was hearsay. The defense needed to bring these witnesses into court if they were going to make a legitimate argument that Laci was alive the morning of the twenty-fourth and that someone else was responsible for her death. Reference was also made to the other pregnant women killed in the area, but the judge similarly instructed the jury to disregard it.

The more disturbing question is what else may have been discovered by the police and never revealed to the defense?

Of all the matters that, under our system of government, are left to be determined in our court, none reach the gravity of those cases where the issue involves the ultimate question of life or death. This determination should never be made under any circumstances other than those providing complete fairness and honesty.

A prosecutor in Arizona was recently disbarred for presenting testimony he knew to be false in a death penalty case.

Section 128 of the California Penal Code provides for the death penalty or life imprisonment without parole for perjury that procures the conviction and execution of any innocent person.

I wonder: What should the penalty be for someone who suppresses evidence that might exonerate an innocent person in a death penalty case?

Harriet Ryan from Court TV reported: "Modesto Police Department detective Al Brocchini, who wept Wednesday as Sharon Rocha described missing her daughter and grandson, broke into a broad smile during the press conference. He and another detective, Jon Buehler, said that it was an inside joke in the department that he and three other detectives at the center of the investigation only had high school diplomas, but the man they were pursuing held a degree from California Polytechnic University."

"He liked to think he was smarter than everybody," Brocchini said. "I want him to know I have a high school diploma only."

What objectivity can be expected from an investigator who both cries and smiles broadly at a press conference involving his case? Detective Buehler told *People* magazine that Scott "did fake sniffles" when shown pictures of the remains of Laci and Conner. Are we to assume that Detective Brocchini shed honest tears when he broke down at the press conference? Why was he even *at* a press conference?

Investigators must be fair and dispassionate in order for the process to work effectively and to ensure public confidence. What mind-set would consider a capital case—a life-or-death matter—to be some sort of matching of wits or a personal contest between the accuser and the accused? This concept has frightening implications and is totally foreign to our criminal justice system.

I won't even try to interpret or comment on what could explain Brocchini's wanting Scott to know that he had not gone beyond high school and choosing a press conference to transmit that message. Clearly, the contest Brocchini had in mind would turn out to be a very unfair one for Scott Peterson.

WHAT THE JURY DIDN'T HEAR

Direct evidence means evidence that directly proves a fact, without an inference or a presumption, and which in itself, if true, conclusively establishes that fact.
—California Evidence Code, Section 410.

It appears the jurors convicted Scott Peterson because they had no other explanation for who murdered Laci and Conner. Several of the jurors commented at a news conference after the trial that they were left with no other possibilities as to who the killer was. "When you add it up, there doesn't appear to be any other option," said one of the jurors.

Six witnesses said that they saw Laci alive the morning of December 24 walking her dog. During the trial, we heard the defense speak the phrase "We have direct evidence."

We did. Unfortunately, that evidence didn't make it to the courtroom.

I repeatedly went through the thousands of pages of reports and police logs, each time with a different focus. When I scoured them looking for suspicious vehicles in Laci's neighborhood at the time she disappeared, two reports stood out.

Robert Nickerson, a building inspector with the City of Modesto, inspected a project at the Medina home across the street from Laci's house about 8:20 A.M. on December 24. He believes that he left the home about 9:20 A.M. and walked to his vehicle, from which he had a clear view of the Peterson home.

He was familiar with Scott and Laci and their home because he had inspected their swimming pool the year before.

When he left the Medinas' home, Nickerson said that he had to drive around a vehicle to get out. He believed that it was a white Ford van that was blocking his way. He recalled that the van had two back doors, and the paint was chipping around the window, revealing the gray primer. He also noted a crude rack on top with wooden cross supports.

About the same time, witness Kristen Dempewolf walked up the same street. As she was passing the house, she noticed what appeared to be the same van parked on the street.

She described the van as an unusually long, older white utility van without rear side windows. The other windows were tinted. As she walked by, she noticed that the upper portion of the van looked oxidized and dull, as if someone had used a scouring pad on it.

It was parked in front of the Medina home, directly across the street from the Peterson house. Dempewolf reported what she saw to the police and told them that she had never seen this van before, although she walked the neighborhood frequently.

This information was not heard by Peterson's jury.

It seems that Dempewolf and Nickerson had independently witnessed the same thing at the same time.

The evidence was starting to connect in my mind: Diana Campos saw two men yelling at Laci. Three of the six witnesses who saw Laci on the morning of December 24 placed her at the same location at the same time, around 10:00 to 10:30 A.M. There were no reported sightings after that.

As I continued poring through the reports and dispatches looking for mentions of suspicious vehicles, I experienced one of the biggest revelations in the disappearance of Laci Peterson.

I found a report from a driving-school instructor, Leora Garcia. She had been training a student in Scott and Laci's neighborhood the morning of December 24. It was only a little mention, a few lines long. Garcia reported that she saw a "vehicle pulled to the side of the road. She noticed a long coat hanging out and it sped off." There is no mention of where this occurred or what the suspicious vehicle looked like. She was able to read part of the license plate.

That's all there was, this short report.

I called Garcia at her home in Ripon, a town not far from Modesto. I verified who she was and that she had been driving around Laci's neighborhood training a student driver the morning of December 24. I asked where she'd seen the suspicious vehicle she reported to the police. She said she saw it near the Moose Park parking lot that was located underneath Stanislaus County Hospital, and I immediately realized this was where Diana Campos saw Laci with the two men following close behind and verbally assaulting her. This was also close to the area where Martha Aguilar and Gene Pedrioli reported seeing her.

Garcia told me that the vehicle was a white van with paint peeling off the sides near the roof and a weird wooden rack on top that she'll never forget. It had Texas license plates with a rainbow frame, she said. When she saw the van, she was making the loop underneath the bridge on La Loma Avenue. Something about the van frightened her.

As the van sped off in front of her, she stopped her car. It was then, she said, that she saw a woman's coat caught in the passenger door. She said a strange feeling came over her and that she was very scared.

This appeared to be the same van that Nickerson and Dempewolf saw. They each separately describe the same details on the van.

Very close to this location there was a police report of screaming heard the morning of December 24 near the public bathrooms in the park. Remember, police dismissed the scream heard as simply being a "rumor."

What was going on in that area at that time was probably the most important thing the police should have focused on. Instead, they focused on Scott Peterson, and these important eyewitnesses were ignored.

One officer took the Garcia statement. A different officer took the statement of Kristen Dempewolf. Yet another person took the statement of building inspector Nickerson. Apparently I was the only one to see the overlap of information from these witnesses.

I believe there's much to suggest that Laci Peterson was abducted. First is the duct tape on Laci's thighs. Next is the caffeine that showed up in Laci's autopsy report. Everyone close to Laci knew that she avoided caffeine during her pregnancy. The fact that she had caffeine in her system could lead us to believe that she must have been in a desperate situation at the end of her life.

Then there's the matter of Laci's shoes. Consider this from

Judge Ricardo Cordova's testimony at trial when being questioned by Geragos. The testimony concerns a pair of shoes that
matched some that Laci had:

> Q. Covena and Edgebrook. Do you know that to be close
> or in the close vicinity of the Petersons' house?
>
> A. It was around the corner from their home.
>
> Q. Approximately how many feet away?
>
> A. I guess about a hundred and fifty feet or so.
>
> Q. Okay. Would it—is it fair to say that you then saw
> some—you observed a pair of women's sandals with a
> flower pattern lying in the roadway there?
>
> A. Yes, I did.
>
> Q. Did you point those out to the detective?
>
> A. I did. They were near the—they were off the pave-
> ment. There's no gutter there, but it looked like it was in
> the grassy area off the pavement into the first—the
> house's yard, and I saw some sandals, flip-flops—looked
> like women's flip-flops to me.
>
> Q. Okay. Did you point those out to Detective Banks?
>
> A. Yes, I did.
>
> Q. Okay. And when you pointed them out to Detective
> Banks, did Detective Banks do anything?

A. He didn't. He left the sandals there.

Q. Okay. And that was what date?

A. That was on Christmas morning. The twenty-fifth of December.

Q. On the twenty-fifth of December? Okay. Did you make any indication that you thought that the sandals might have something to do with anything?

A. I—I think I made a comment: I wonder if these have anything to do with that.

Q. With what?

A. With Ms. Peterson's disappearance.

. . .

Q. And did Detective Banks pick these shoes up?

A. No, he didn't.

The shoes weren't the only articles to turn up. Four blocks away from the Peterson home, a resident found a pair of women's gloves in the street. I obtained this information from a police phone log. There was apparently no follow-up to the call.

I don't think we can overlook the fact that there were numerous crimes in the area at the time of Laci's disappearance. Nor can we ignore the police report from the other pregnant woman who was terrorized about the same time.

How and where was Laci abducted? Was it while interrupting the Todd burglary at the Medina house? Was it from the public bathroom outside the hospital parking lot where a woman's scream was heard? Was she taken away in the white van that a witness saw speed away from the park area where Laci was last seen, apparently the same white van that was across from the Peterson house just forty-five minutes earlier that same morning?

The police didn't investigate the leads and witnesses, and the defense didn't present them.

One fact problematic to the defense was that the bodies of Laci and Conner were found where Scott was fishing. Was it possible that someone planted the bodies near Berkeley after hearing Scott had been fishing there? I always believed it was a possibility, considering that it was reported early on in the case by the media that Peterson had been fishing near Berkeley.

Witnesses reported a suspicious white van and a suspicious brown van in the Petersons' neighborhood. What if one of these distinct-looking vehicles was caught on video in Berkeley?

A professor from the University of California at Berkeley was conducting an ongoing traffic study in the Berkeley area. He mounted twelve cameras on top of an apartment complex. His cameras recorded the activity on the local highways. He apparently ran the video all day and all night. The tapes were then converted to computer files and saved as study data.

On January 27, 2003, Detective Brocchini contacted the professor in an attempt to get a copy of his video from December 24. Brocchini wrote in an e-mail to the professor, "Even with bad resolution, we may be able to see what is in the boat and open truck bed when it goes by. Right now we need a break, and you may be able to supply it. Thanks for checking."

The professor responded via e-mail, "I don't think the resolution is good enough for that purpose. For example, we cannot figure out the makers of vehicles. We can roughly figure out colors and types (passenger car or SUV)."

It seems to me it would also be worth knowing if brown or white vans could have been identified. This question was never asked.

During my investigation, I made several attempts to acquire videotapes from the professor. Eventually the footage was seized by the FBI and never viewed by the defense.

Finally, there were the six other pregnant women who disappeared within three years of Laci's murder and within eighty miles of Modesto. Two of them ended up in the San Francisco Bay outside of Berkeley with their hands, feet, and heads missing; they disappeared on special satanic days. Coincidence? I don't think so.

I think it's entirely possible that Laci was another one on this list who disappeared suddenly because she had been abducted.

Circumstantial evidence is defined by California Jury Instructions Criminal 2.0 as "evidence that, if found to be true, proves a fact from which an inference of the existence of another fact may be drawn."

Nickerson and Dempewolf saw the suspicious white van,

with its distinct features, parked across from the Peterson home the morning Laci disappeared.

The morning of December 24, Laci was seen walking with her dog on her usual route. Six credible witnesses saw her. The last witness to see Laci said she was being followed by two men yelling and cursing at her. McKenzie, her dog, was upset by these two men. At the same time and location, a witness saw the same white van speed away.

Three suspicious vehicles—the brown van, the white van, and the white sedan—were parked across the street from Laci's house. A residential burglary was in progress. Criminals from the airport district were all over her neighborhood.

I think there is strong circumstantial evidence that Laci was abducted the morning of the twenty-fourth, probably from the park area where she was last seen.

The jury never heard from any of these witnesses. Dempewolf, Nickerson, and Garcia never testified at the trial.

A serious issue in the case involved demonstrative evidence to establish whether or not Scott Peterson could have disposed of Laci's body from his boat, as contended by the prosecution.

Under California law, evidence in the form of an experiment is relevant if the experiment has any tendency in reason to prove or disprove any disputed fact that is of consequence to the determination of an issue.

During their deliberations, the jury asked to view the boat, which was located in the courthouse parking lot. The judge allowed the jurors to get into the boat to help them determine whether Laci's body could have been handled as claimed by the prosecution. The jurors went beyond what the judge had authorized by jumping up and down and rocking the boat back and forth. This, of course, was totally unlike testing the boat while it was afloat rather than in a parking lot.

The judge denied Geragos's motion for a mistrial based on the jurors' conduct.

The prosecution's theory was that Scott dumped Laci's 145-pound body out of his 14-foot boat with an 8-pound anchor attached to her limbs. It seemed like an impossible scenario. At the trial, the Modesto detectives admitted that they had talked about doing their own experiment and asked the district attorney's office for permission. They were told no.

If they had done that test and it failed, they would have been obligated, pursuant to the law, to give the results of their test over to the defense. It would have probably failed, in my opinion, and would have dealt a damaging blow to the prosecution's theory of how Laci's body ended up in the bay.

Geragos argued vigorously that it was impossible to push a 150-pound body with weights overboard from Scott's 14-foot aluminum boat without it capsizing.

The following document represents in part the defense motion for a new trial regarding this issue:

IX. THE TRIAL COURT ERRED BY EXCLUDING DEMONSTRATIVE EVIDENCE—A VIDEOTAPED EXPERIMENT SHOWING THE INSTABILITY OF THE BOAT—OFFERED BY THE DEFENSE.

A. Background Facts

Throughout its case, the prosecution contended that Mr. Peterson disposed of Laci's body in the San Francisco Bay on or about December 24, 2002. More specifically, the prosecution contended that Mr. Peterson was able to dispose of the 150-pound body with four weights estimated at 8 pounds each attached to the body, out of a 14-foot boat without the boat overturning in the rough waters of the bay, allowing Mr. Peterson a safe return to shore. The defense consistently attempted to point out the impossibility of the prosecution theory. Simply put, Mr. Peterson could not have dumped Laci's body with weights attached from the 14-foot boat amidst the high currents of the bay without the boat overturning or capsizing.

In order to conclusively prove the impossibility of the prosecution's theory of the case, the defense decided to conduct the one experiment the prosecution refused to do. On October 16, 2004, the defense replicated what, according to the prosecution, had allegedly taken place in the San Francisco Bay. The defense had earlier purchased a 14-foot Gamefisher aluminum boat, identical to the one allegedly used by Mr. Peterson. For the experiment, the defense placed this boat near Brooks Island in *the San Francisco Bay, which was the area where the prosecution's experts testified that Laci's body was disposed. The testing was videotaped by Nareg Gourjian, a lawyer employed by defense attorney Mark J. Geragos. While being videotaped, Raffi Naljian, another employee of the defense attorney, threw overboard a dummy with four weights attached to it into the bay. For purposes of the experiment, Mr. Naljian was similar in size and weight as Mr. Peterson.* The dummy used was similar in weight to Laci and had four weights estimated at 8 pounds each attached to it. The boat was identical to that owned by Mr. Peterson, and contained the same items, i.e., tackle box, anchors, and weights, as the prosecution alleged were in Mr. Peterson's boat in December 2002. Most importantly, the seas were calmer in October 2004, when the experiment was conducted, than they had been in December 2002, when the alleged crime occurred. (This was confirmed by prosecution expert, Dr. Ralph Cheng.)*

During the first attempt to throw the dummy out of the boat, the boat overturned, leaving Mr. Naljian stranded in the water.

---

* Mr. Naljian weighed approximately 178 pounds the morning of the experiment and wore a weight belt making him a total of 198 pounds, the weight of Mr. Peterson in December 2002.

After a brief hearing on the admissibility of the videotape of this experiment, the trial court excluded it on the grounds that the weather conditions during the experiment were not substantially similar to those in December 2002, the boat used in the experiment was not the actual boat used by Mr. Peterson, the experiment was conducted by an employee of the defense attorney, and there was no testimony as to how the body was actually disposed of from the boat. When defense counsel objected that the reasons cited by the court were not sufficient grounds to exclude the experiment, the judge responded, "I don't have to explain my damn rulings. I made my rulings. I made this ruling, and that's the ruling, period. All right. I'm not giving you the boat, either."

The persons conducting the experiment all could have been cross-examined if the video had been admitted. Whether or not this was prejudicial error is a matter for the appeals process.

Strictly as a matter of commentary, however, it seems to me that a jury intelligent enough to decide if a young man should live or die should be intelligent enough to reach their own conclusion after hearing testimony regarding weather conditions on two dates, knowing that it was not the same boat, and knowing that the defense lawyer's employees conducted the experiment.

Geragos went from saying that he would prove Scott was "stone cold innocent" to saying in his closing statement, "I would love nothing more, and I mean this, than to solve this case and to point to somebody and say this is who did this. But the fact of the matter is that they have not proved this case; they have not proved that Scott Peterson did anything except lie."

It should not have been the burden of the defense to prove the identity of the actual killer or killers.

In my opinion, if the jury had heard all of the relevant information related to the case, Scott Peterson would not be on death row today.

12

BEYOND THE VERDICT

I sat in front of the television November 12, 2004, and watched as Scott Peterson's verdict was announced, and the crowd outside cheered. My wife began to sob. I felt almost physically ill.

Not long after, I received a phone call from Jackie and Lee Peterson. They were driving back to San Diego, and they had questions. What had gone wrong? What had happened to the evidence and the witnesses I'd uncovered?

A trial is supposed to be a search for the truth. In my opinion, the police and prosecution were overzealous in what appeared to me to be a very weak case. This trial had not been about justice; it had been a contest.

It was apparent in the way the police trickled the discovery to us. It was even more clear in the way they didn't appear to follow up on leads. Many pieces of physical evidence that may have helped the defense no longer exist: the tape (or seaweed, as they claim) on the baby's ear, the nooselike tape wound around the baby's neck and chest, the professor's videotape in Berkeley, the videotape at Salon Salon from the night of December 23, the Croton watch that was pawned days after Laci's disappearance, the recorded phone conversation from state prison about burglar Steve Todd's confronting Laci during the Medina burglary, the videotape of the woman throwing the stolen jewelry from the Medinas back into the Modesto Police Department, even the safe taken from the Medina house.

I had hand delivered a letter written by Susan Medina to Detective Grogan asking for her safe to be returned, as per her request. We were informed that her safe was destroyed by the police—and with it, any possible fingerprint evidence.

CONVICTION BY MEDIA

There's no doubt that coverage of the case affected the verdict. Scott was portrayed as guilty from the beginning, and the Amber Frey news—announced at a Modesto police press conference—sealed his fate. His public demeanor didn't help. If he was stone-faced, he was branded a sociopath. If he showed emotion, he was faking it.

As talk-show lawyers pondered his future, Scott Peterson easily became the most hated man in America.

Photographs of Laci, the pretty young woman with a dazzling smile, brought forth an outpouring of public sympathy. More than one thousand people attended a candlelight vigil for her on December 31, 2002. TV broadcaster Bill O'Reilly was quoted in *Vanity Fair* as saying, "We do Laci Peterson every fifteen minutes and see the numbers go up."

When Laci Peterson was on the cover, *People* magazine sales soared. Media coverage of her murder and Scott Peterson's trial turned a tragedy into an event of us versus them, complete with cheering fans at the trial and jurors holding press conferences.

There may have been no cameras allowed in the courtroom, but that didn't stop *E! True Hollywood Story* from broadcasting Laci's story. It didn't stop USA Network's *The Perfect Husband*, which Jeff Wachtel, USA's executive vice president of original scripted programming, called, "a movie about our culture— how someone can gain then betray the trust of a woman, a family, a community."

The public was hungry for Peterson news, and the media provided it, sometimes unwisely. Almost everyone with an opinion became an expert.

Boston Globe columnist Renee Graham wrote: "If attorneys have long been saddled with reputations as ambulance-chasing ghouls, the Peterson case has recast them as camera-hogging fools. Except for CNN's classy legal analyst Jeffrey Toobin, most TV appearances by lawyers commenting on the case have been tantamount to 'Crossfire'-style smackdowns offering more volume than thoughtful perspective. Intended to add pertinent insights, these sessions usually resembled the kinds of blockhead arguments found in sports bars in the wee hours." Even I got to where I didn't think I could watch another pundit commenting on the case.

POLICE TOOL

The Peterson case was not the first high-profile case where Modesto police worked with national media. Chandra Levy, who disappeared April 30, 2001, in Washington, D.C., and whose remains were later found there, was the subject of extensive media coverage, primarily because of her purported romantic relationship with Congressman Gary Condit.

To analyze the unexpected feeding frenzy over a missing-persons case, the nonprofit research organization Center for Media and Public Affairs examined the media coverage from first reports on May 16, 2001, through August 8, 2001, from four major newspapers, two twenty-four-hour cable news channels, and the evening and (for July only) morning news shows of the major broadcast networks. Overall they tallied 739 stories or program segments on the Chandra Levy–Gary Condit story.

According to CMPA, Condit was the most joked-about person in America that July.

> *Throughout July, he was the target of 95 jokes by late-night TV comedians, a figure that surpassed the combined totals of his three nearest competitors—George W. Bush (42), Bill Clinton (31) and Dick Cheney (18). No other individual was the target of more than four jokes that month. That batch of barbs left him as the third leading joke target of 2001 with 123 jokes to his credit (or debit), a total surpassed only by Bill Clinton (529) and George W. Bush (448). Comedians also found Bill Clinton and Gary Condit an irresistible combination that frequently let them skewer two targets with a single dart.*

Although Condit was never a suspect in Chandra Levy's death, he was unofficially convicted because of his relationship with her. Modesto police apparently discovered the power of the national media with that case. Condit's career was ruined. The last I read about him, he and his children were trying to start up an ice-cream franchise while they sued those who had contributed to that unofficial conviction that only ended when the terrorist attacks of September 11, 2001, focused our nation's attention on a real danger.

With the Peterson case, the media—and Modesto—had another cheating husband. And as was the case with Condit, and in the 1950s, Sam Sheppard, the bias played out with the familiar theme: "He was unfaithful, so he must have killed her."

Rumors made it to the media, from the tabloids up. The stories about the blood on the mop and the multiple anchors—both untrue—somehow made it to the public via the media, just to name two. These rumors and the massive publicity surrounding the case contributed to Scott Peterson's conviction. It seems inconceivable that the jury pool wasn't in some way prejudiced by the false information reported by much of the media early in the case.

SAM SHEPPARD SIMILARITIES

Long before Scott Peterson was arrested for killing his wife and tried by the media with help of the police, Dr. Sam Sheppard was engaged in an eerily similar case in 1954.

The basis for *The Fugitive*'s Richard Kimble, whose wife was killed by "a one-armed man," Sheppard was accused of the 1954 murder of his wife. Within four hours on the scene, the police decided that Sheppard was the only suspect and refused to believe his story about seeing a "bushy-haired man" escaping.

The press printed police detective Robert Schottke's comment "I think you are the one who killed your wife" as if it were fact. They wrote about Sheppard's lover and searched for others. Newspaper editorials attacked the police for not being aggressive enough, and the *Cleveland Press* ran a front-page editorial titled "Somebody Is Getting Away with Murder."

The coroner questioned Sheppard on national television and had Sheppard's lawyer ejected from the hearing because he interrupted with certain procedural objections.

The media was also allowed to look on and report as the police were interrogating Sheppard and searching his home and were given evidence by the prosecution that would not have been admissible at trial—but which they printed as fact, thereby bringing it to the attention of future jurors.

The media feeds public appetites, and the public was hungry for anything resembling news about the Peterson case. Jeering crowds greeted Scott Peterson as he was first led to the Modesto jail. Almost anyone who owns a television witnessed the public celebration the day the verdict was read.

Peterson stories continued to circulate. There's the real estate agent who bought Scott and Laci's home for $10,000 over the asking price and then found a ten-inch knife in a void in the patio cabinet the Petersons used to store a small refrigerator. He reported this to a tabloid magazine only days after the magazine incorrectly printed that Laci's throat had been slit. The agent was then fired from his position because of interviews he gave to the *Modesto Bee* and two Sacramento television news stations.

There's even a market for Peterson memorabilia, *Newsday* reports. Seven months after Scott's conviction, a note he wrote on the back of a business card was auctioned at the Americana auction held by Leland's of Seaford, New York. The note, which Scott left under a windshield wiper of a car that had a flyer about Laci on its dashboard, read, "Thank you for having Laci's picture on your car. Scott."

The high bid? $666.

Scott Peterson now occupies a cell on San Quentin State Prison's death row with more than 640 other condemned inmates. The entire case of Scott Peterson is surrounded by uncertainty.

If Peterson murdered his wife and unborn child with premeditation and malice aforethought, what was his motive?

And how could this fertilizer salesman who so bungled his actions after his wife's disappearance so cleverly commit this crime, leaving no eyewitnesses and no physical evidence other than a single strand of hair that provided no reasonable basis to support any inference of guilt?

Where did these murders take place? How did they take place?

What motive could have caused such a heinous crime by someone who had never in his thirty years evidenced any criminal tendencies?

Could it be that a bizarre chain of circumstances caused a jury to believe an innocent man guilty of double murder and deserving of the death penalty?

There is no question that there were suspicious circumstances. Prominent among these was Peterson's story that he had gone fishing on the day of Laci's disappearance in the same bay where Laci's body and the fetus of their unborn son were subsequently located. The media pounced on this. Explanations may seem improbable or unlikely but still do not provide a permissible inference from that fact alone of guilt.

Less suspicious but probably more damning was his adulterous liaison with Amber Frey, with whom he had three dates. Yet she was consistently described in the press as his mistress and presented as his motive for murdering his pregnant wife. No serious evidence supported this theory, yet it undoubtedly was the cause of great prejudice and even hostility throughout the community. It established him as immoral and untrustworthy, and though it had no real relevance to the crime itself, it may have cost him the verdict.

Peterson himself engaged in conduct that aroused suspicion with good reason: his dyed hair, the cash on his person when he was arrested, and what some perceived as an inadequate display of grief or sufficient participation in the search following Laci's disappearance. Of course, the argument can equally be made that a clever criminal would have acted quite the opposite and adopted a pose of grief and made heroic efforts in the search activities.

Really, Peterson couldn't get a break. The media commentaries constantly charged fakery whenever he displayed emotion or tears during the trial.

Regardless of one's interpretations of these matters, they

would appear to fall markedly short of logically supplying evidence necessary to establish proof of murder. Suspicion and proof are entirely different concepts.

We cannot say with any certainty what prejudices the massive media coverage caused. It even resulted in Congress renaming the Unborn Victims of Violence Act Laci and Conner's Law. The bill, which is opposed by prochoice groups, defines an unborn fetus as a person and aims to punish violence against women more severely when that violence injures or terminates a pregnancy. Never in our history has such prejudicial material targeted a criminal proceeding.

No one can reasonably say that such pervasive media attention has no effect on juries. How can this prevailing atmosphere be reconciled with the concept of jurors being admonished by the court to insulate themselves from all such sources because they are untrustworthy?

Consider the following:

Within a span of twelve years, California has been the scene of three celebrated murder trials wherein defendants have been accused of the murder of their present or former spouses. All trials were surrounded by massive publicity. Two, O. J. Simpson and Robert Blake, largely because of the notoriety of the principals, and the third, Scott Peterson, largely because of the sensationalism of the crime: the death of his attractive young wife and his unborn child. All were tried by juries all under the same California laws. Only Scott Peterson was convicted.

In the Simpson case, the time, place, and manner of death were clear. There had been a long history of marital discord. The physical evidence was strong. Simpson's blood was found at the scene as well as hair matching his in a cap nearby. A glove stained with blood was found at the scene and its mate located by Simpson's house. The two victims' hair and blood were found on the glove. Simpson's own blood was tracked into his house and bathroom. There was additional incriminating physical evidence, including cuts on Simpson's hands.

He did not testify at the trial. The jury found him not guilty after less than five hours of deliberation. A subsequent civil-trial jury, on basically the same evidence, found by a preponderance of the evidence that he had killed his wife and her companion.

In March 2005, a Los Angeles jury found Robert Blake not guilty of killing his wife, Bonny Lee Bakley. She was shot to death in Blake's car, which was parked near a restaurant where the couple had eaten dinner. The story was that he had left her while he went back to the restaurant to recover his handgun, which he had inadvertently left. When he returned to his car, he found his bleeding wife.

There was evidence that Blake had asked two different individuals to kill his wife, that he hated her, and that on the night of her death, he did not act as one would expect from a grief-stricken husband.

Blake also was found not guilty. The murder weapon was found in a trash bin. It was not the one he said he had retrieved from the restaurant. The jurors felt the prosecution had failed to link Blake to the gun used in the crime and that the evidence was insufficient to convict.

Following a reversal during the appellate process, it is not unusual for the same case with the same evidence to be tried before a different jury and result in a completely different verdict. Nevertheless, trial lawyers are the strongest supporters of the jury system. They believe that for the most part jurors take their oath seriously and do their very best to be fair, impartial, and conscientious in the discharge of their duty.

That is far from saying that juries are always right. They are human, and determining the outcome of a case is not science. Jurors can differ in their perceptions, subconscious prejudices, and the way they process information.

The same applies to the witnesses from whom the jurors must ascertain the facts. It is not uncommon for witnesses to become partisans on behalf of the side that calls them.

As I have shown, juries are not always provided with all the information that may relate to the issues in controversy. I believe it is likely that a new trial developing further suggested areas of investigation and unresolved questions and mysterious circumstances could result in Scott Peterson's acquittal.

THE APPEAL

The appeal process following the imposition of a death sentence is lengthy and complicated. The appeal from a death sentence is automatic in the state system under California law. The appeal goes directly to the California Supreme Court, bypassing the district courts. The appeal to the California Supreme Court is not a new trial. Instead, it is an examination of the trial record to determine whether errors of law were committed and if so whether those errors were prejudicial (that is, may have affected the outcome of the trial).

The prisoner cannot waive the automatic appeal to the California Supreme Court.

In hearing the appeal, the Supreme Court does not decide innocence or guilt. Members of the court do not consider if they would have reached the same decision as the jury. They only consider if the jury could have reached their verdict based on the evidence presented to them.

By law in California, the inmate is entitled to have qualified counsel appointed to handle his appeal and also what is designated a habeas corpus proceeding. Usually, separate lawyers are appointed for these two proceedings. This is a right that may be waived only by the inmate's express written agreement.

The habeas corpus proceeding permits additional evidence to be submitted. In this way, matters not contained in the record of the trial court may be raised.

The final decision of the California Supreme Court may be appealed to the United States Supreme Court, but it very infrequently will take these cases.

The habeas corpus proceeding takes place while the

automatic appeal is proceeding. If there is a factual dispute regarding a material fact outside the record, a hearing may be conducted before a referee appointed by the court. The referee's findings are reviewed by the Supreme Court and considered in its decision.

If the results are unsuccessful in the California court system, a petition for habeas corpus may then be filed in the United States Federal District Court. This court will consider any constitutional claims and is empowered to overturn either the conviction, death penalty, or both. This decision may be appealed to the United States Court of Appeals. The last remedy available through the court system would be a final petition to the United States Supreme Court, which, again, would rarely be granted.

The last possible effort would be a request for clemency from the governor of California.

The most recent execution in California occurred in January 2005. The inmate had been on death row for twenty years and ten months.

FINAL THOUGHTS

No one can now say with certainty that Scott Peterson is guilty just as I cannot say with certainty that he is innocent. I can say with certainty that there are too many unresolved questions and mysterious circumstances. There is too much the jury never heard. The eyewitnesses who could have established his innocence were never presented.

It would be disingenuous for me to say I have not become personally involved with this case. I obviously have because of the strong beliefs I have presented.

What if the jury had heard about everything that I knew? Would it have made a difference?

APPENDIX

TIMELINE

November 20, 2002

Amber Frey and Scott Peterson begin affair.

December 24, 2002

Laci Peterson is reported missing.

December 26, 2002

Police serve a search warrant on the Peterson home.

December 30, 2002

Fresno massage therapist Amber Frey contacts Modesto police regarding her affair with Peterson.

January 24, 2003

Addressing a news conference, Amber Frey reveals that she was having an affair with Scott Peterson.

January 28, 2003

Scott Peterson admits on national TV that he had an extramarital affair but says he had nothing to do with his wife's disappearance.

February 18, 2003

With a second search warrant, police officers remove ninety-five items from the Peterson home.

March 5, 2003

Modesto police announce that they are treating the Peterson investigation as a homicide case.

April 13, 2003

The remains of a male infant are found on the shore of San Francisco Bay.

April 14, 2003

A decapitated female body washes up on the shore of San Francisco Bay, near where the infant's body was found.

April 18, 2003

The bodies are identified as those of Laci and Conner Peterson. Scott Peterson is arrested in San Diego.

April 21, 2003

In Stanislaus County Superior Court, Scott Peterson is charged with two felony counts of murder with premeditation and special circumstances. He pleads not guilty.

June 26, 2003

A California Superior Court judge orders that 176 wiretaps of Peterson's telephone calls must be given to the defense.

August 6, 2003

Defense attorneys say Peterson was offered a plea bargain and threatened with the death penalty three months before he was charged.

September 26, 2003

Matt Dalton leaves the Peterson case.

November 17, 2003

The judge binds Peterson over for trial on murder charges in both deaths.

December 3, 2003

Peterson pleads not guilty.

January 8, 2004

Girolami permits a change of venue.

February 2, 2004

Judge Alfred Delucchi bars cameras from the San Mateo County courtroom for the duration of the trial.

March 4, 2004

Jury selection begins.

May 27, 2004

Jury selection is completed. There are six men, six women, and six alternates.

June 1, 2004

The trial of Scott Peterson begins.

June 18, 2004

Juror No. 5, Justin Falconer, says something to Brent Rocha, the brother of Laci Peterson, as the two pass through a security checkpoint at the entrance to the courthouse.

June 21, 2004

Judge Delucchi tells jurors that they must make certain that their actions in and around the courtroom are not misconstrued.

June 23, 2004

Juror No. 5, Justin Falconer, is dismissed from the jury.

August 10, 2004

Amber Frey testifies that Peterson told her he was a widower. Jurors begin hearing recordings of her taped conversations with Peterson.

August 24, 2004

Frey finishes testifying.

October 5, 2004

The prosecution rests.

October 26, 2004

The defense rests.

November 1, 2004

The prosecution makes its closing arguments.

November 2, 2004

The defense makes its closing arguments.

November 3, 2004

Jury deliberations begin.

November 9, 2004

A juror is replaced by an alternate.

November 10, 2004

The alternate juror who replaced Falconer is replaced by an alternate.

November 12, 2004

The jury finds Scott Peterson guilty on both counts.

December 13, 2004

The jury sentences Scott Peterson to death.

ACKNOWLEDGMENTS

I am extremely grateful for the love and support of my family throughout the writing of this book: my wife, Franki, and my children, Cassidy and Joe; my parents, Shirley and Doug Dalton; and my brothers, Bart and Jack Dalton. Thanks to Brad Shoemaker, a real friend. Thanks to Mike Gudgell for continuing the search for truth. Thanks to Bonnie Hearn Hill for her invaluable assistance. The team at Atria Books deserves special recognition. Thank you Judith Curr, Justin Loeber, Isolde Sauer, and Wendy Walker. Finally, thanks to our editor, Peter Borland, and our agent, Laura Dail, for going above and beyond to make this book a reality.

ABOUT THE AUTHOR

Matt Dalton spent thirteen years as a prosecutor involved in all aspects of criminal litigation with the Long Beach City Prosecutor's office and the Los Angeles County District Attorney's office. In 2003, he left the DA's office and joined the firm of Geragos & Geragos. Soon after, he met with his first client: accused murderer Scott Peterson. Matt Dalton earned degrees from UCLA and Loyola Law School and, while working as a prosecutor, received commendations for outstanding contributions to domestic violence prosecutions. He is currently in private practice in Los Angeles.

Bonnie Hearn Hill is a California-based writer and a former newspaper editor.